I0489417

Introduction.

Adult coloring books in a rapidly growing craze around the world. In today's modern world, people are looking to unplug from their phones, tablets, and computers, and do something simple and fun. Coloring for adults is a great stress reliever and it helps you to be calm after a hectic day.

With the mandalas there is no wrong or right way to color them. Just pick whatever colors come to mind and have fun. It really is that easy and fun. Use colored pencils, pastels, crayons, markers, even watercolor paints! Only your imagination can run wild and feel free to experiment with many different mediums.

These amazing tubular mandalas takes it to the next level of fun!

If you enjoyed this coloring book please leave a review on Amazon, or wherever you purchased the book from. To learn more about other coloring books, please visit our website at: http://www.ColoringforGrownUps.net.

Thanks once again, enjoy the book and have fun!

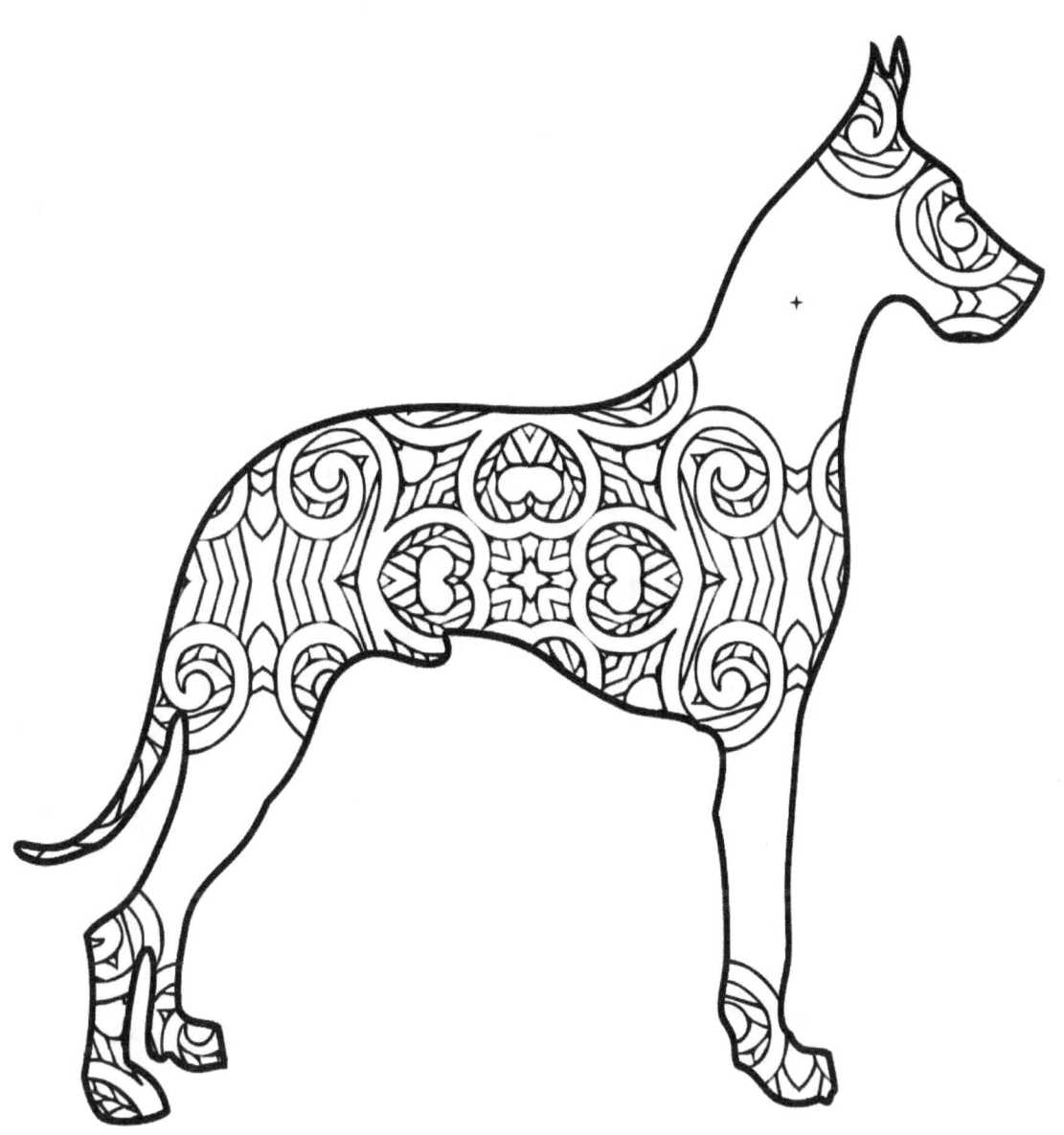

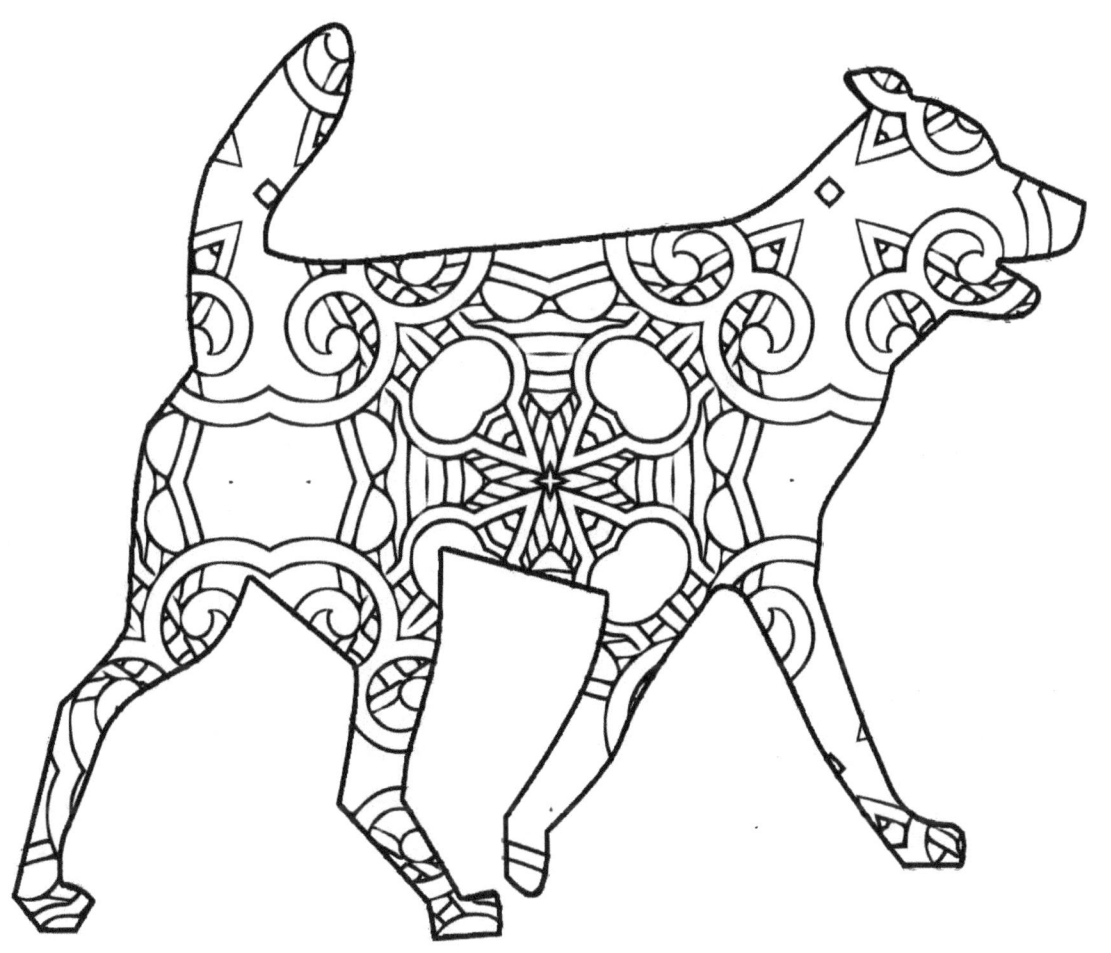

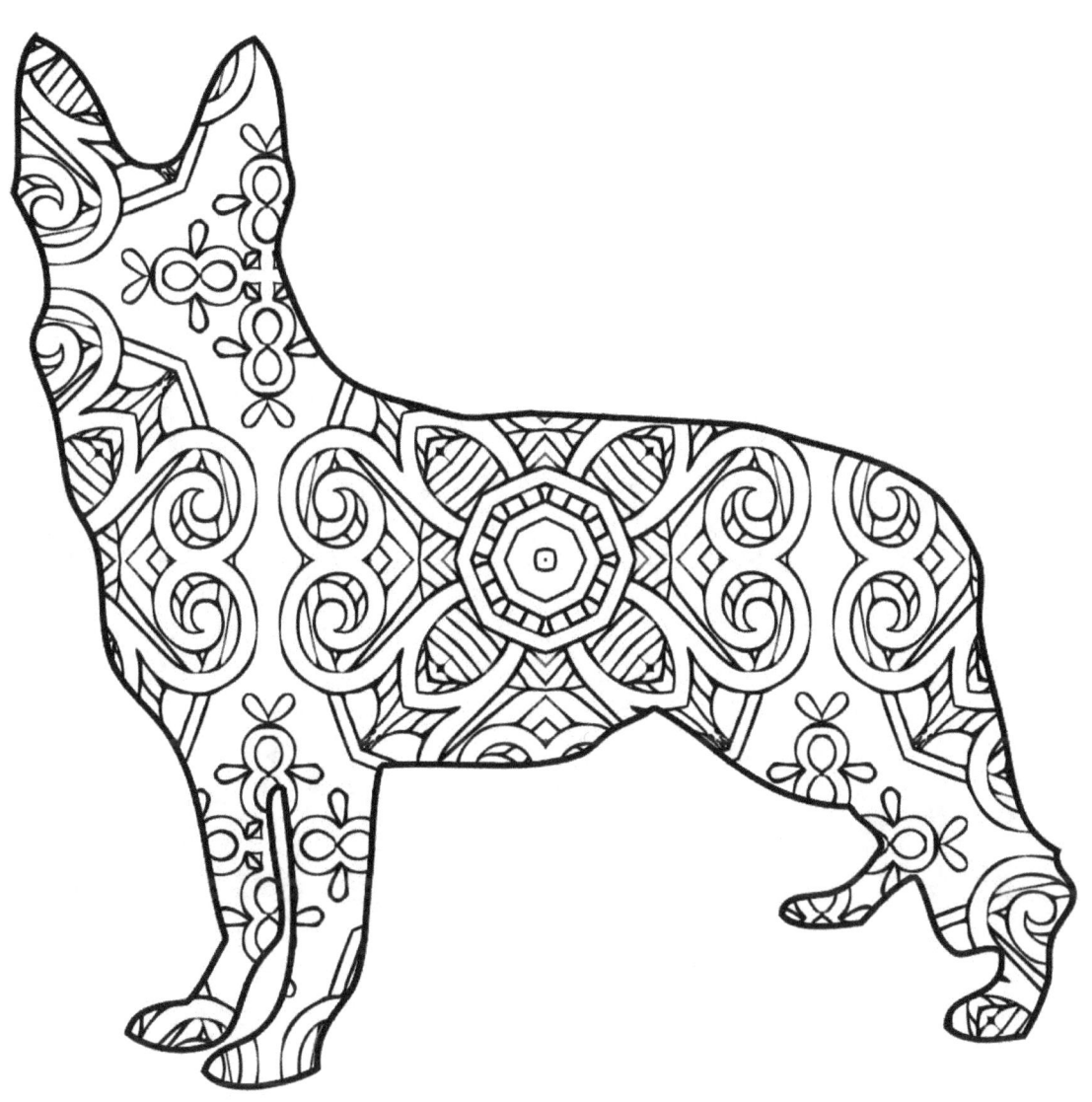

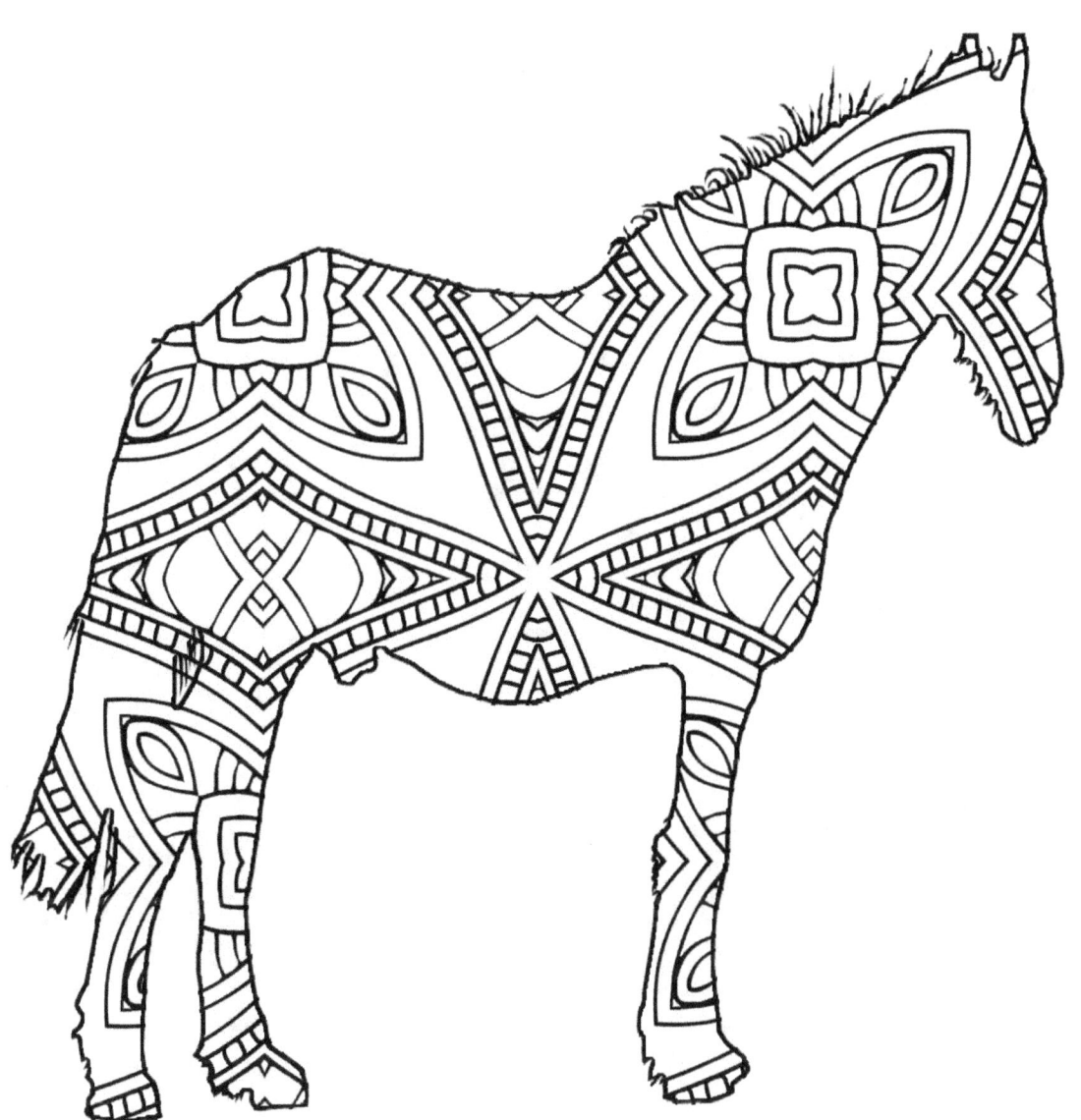

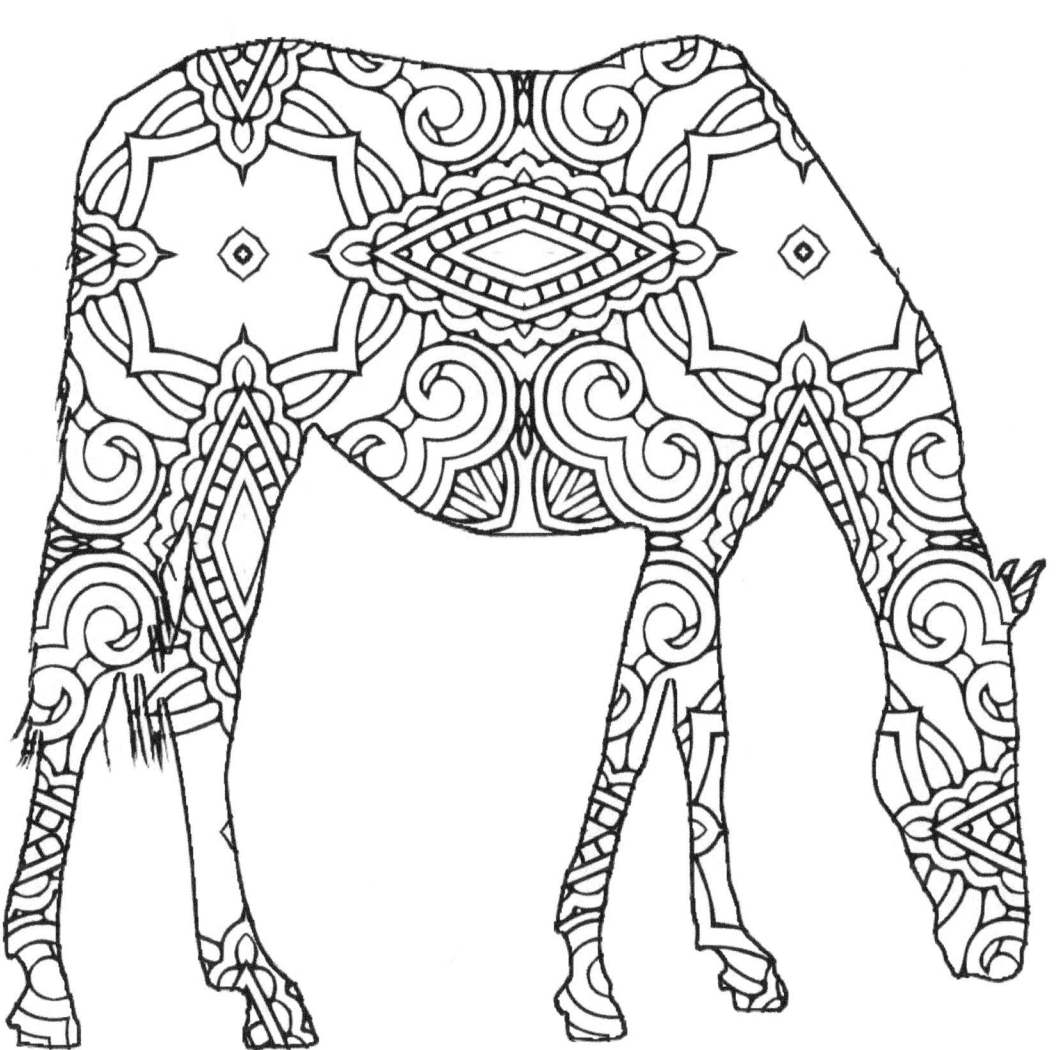

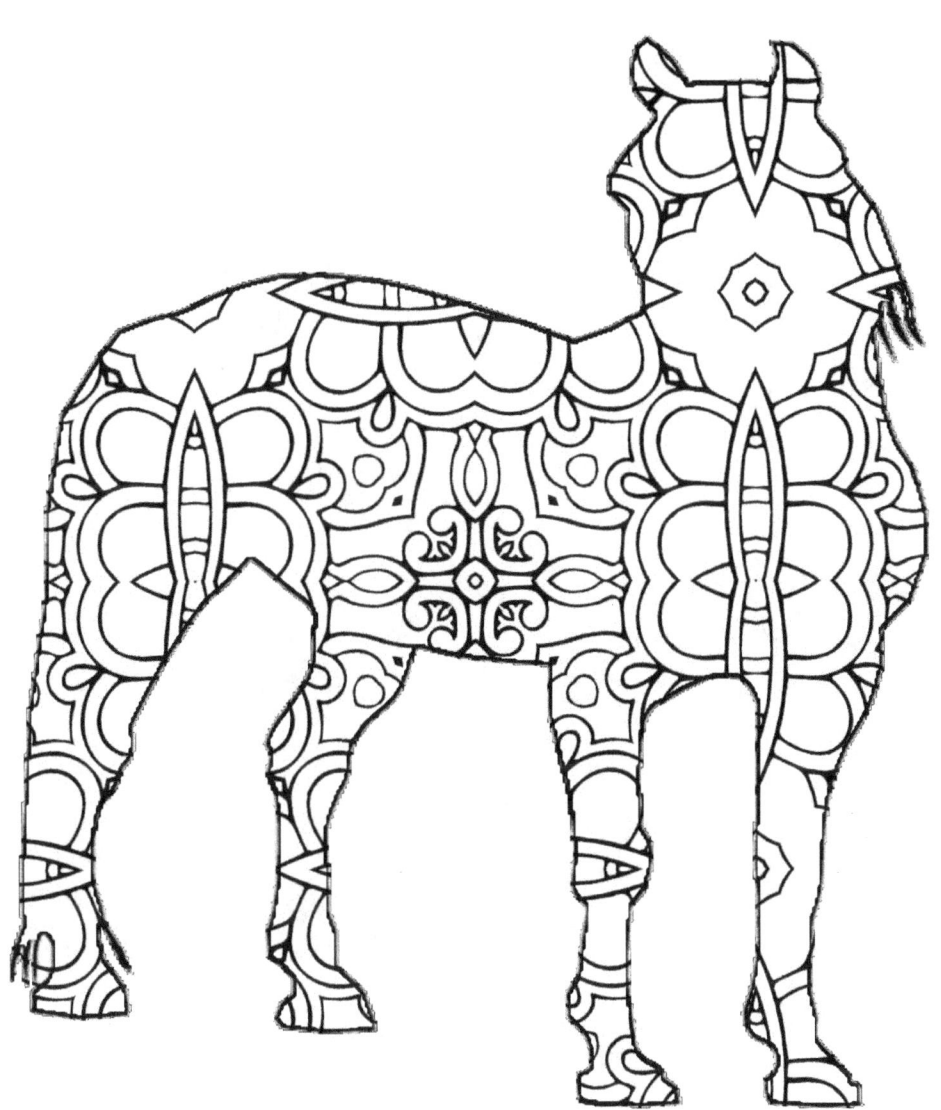

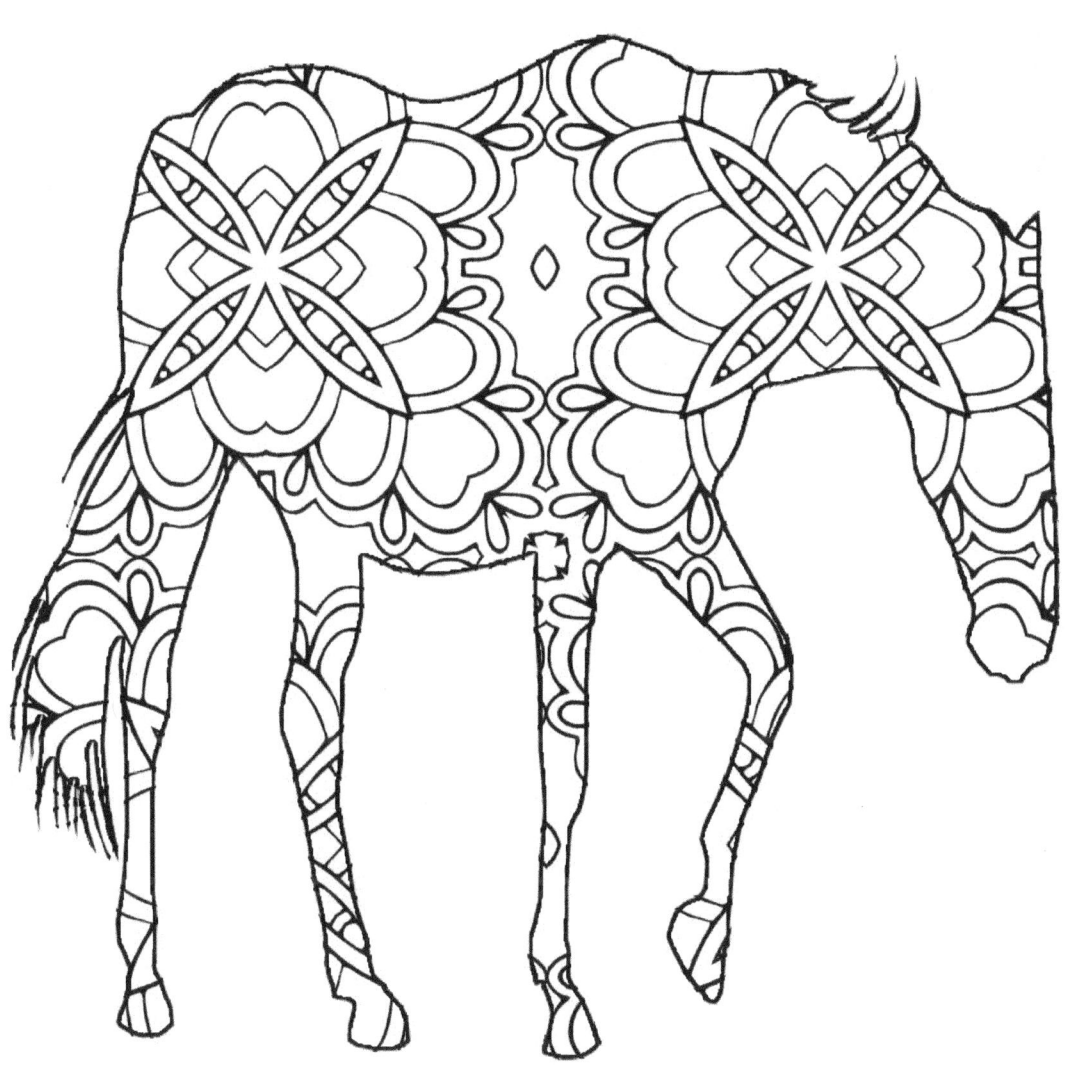

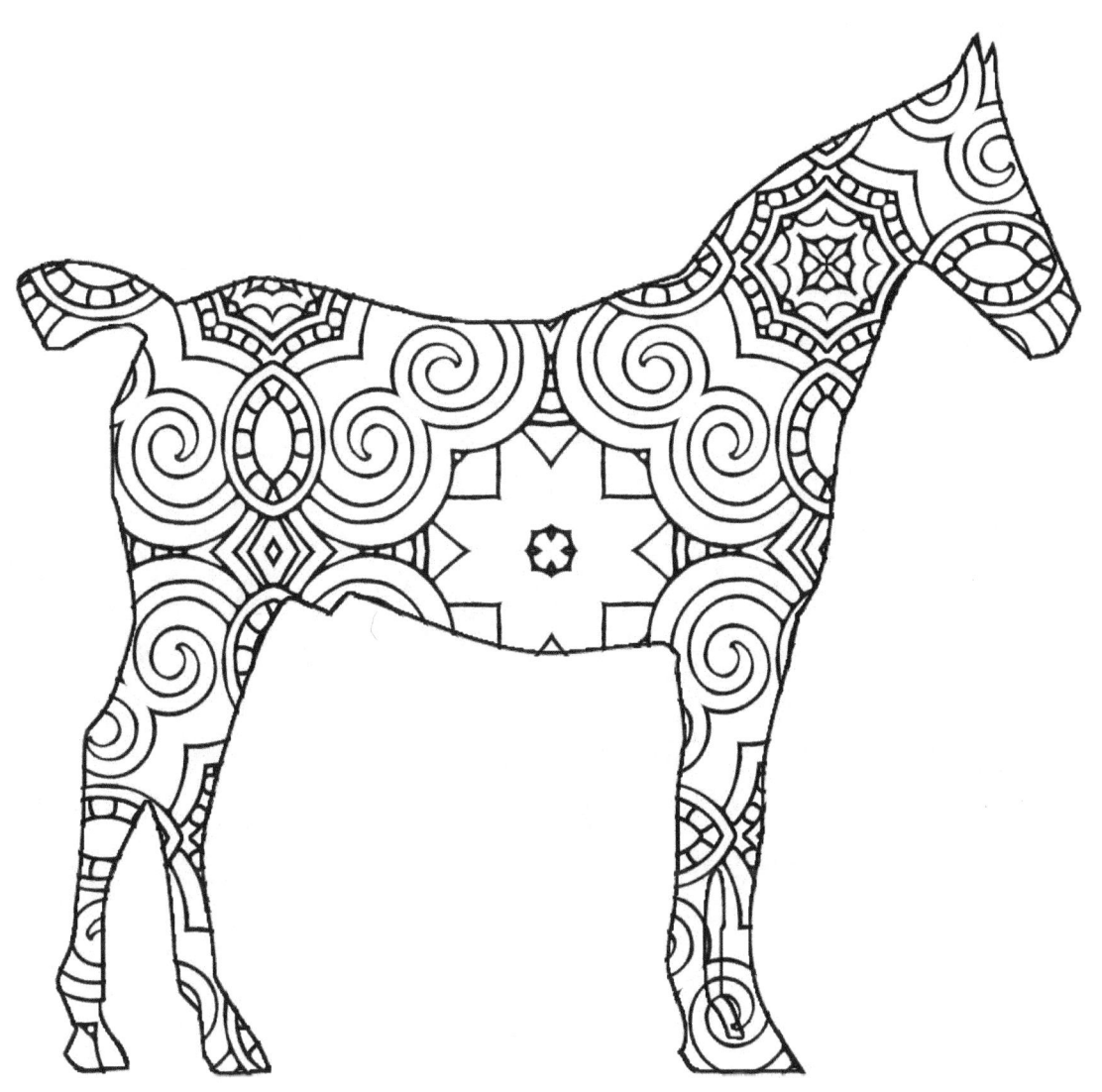

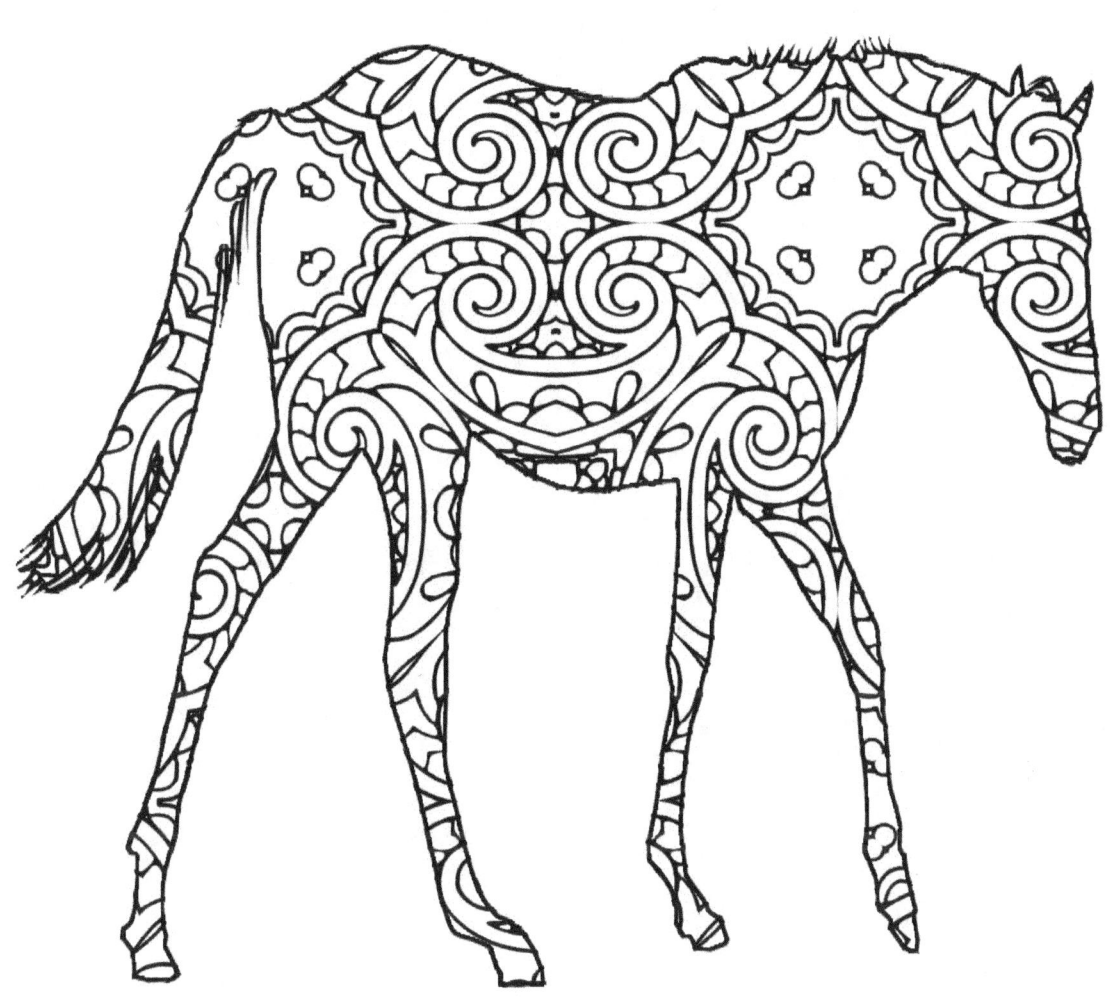

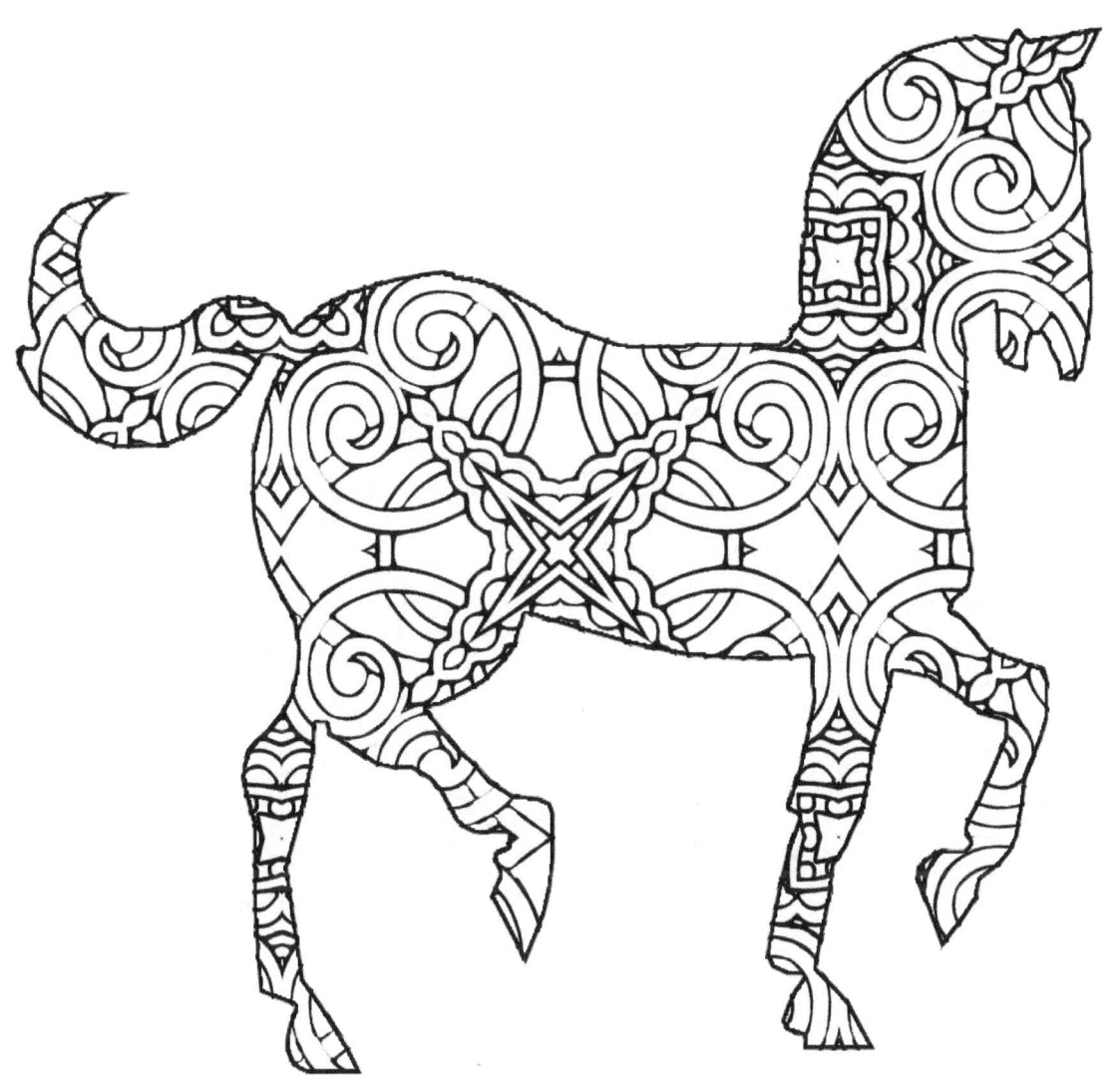

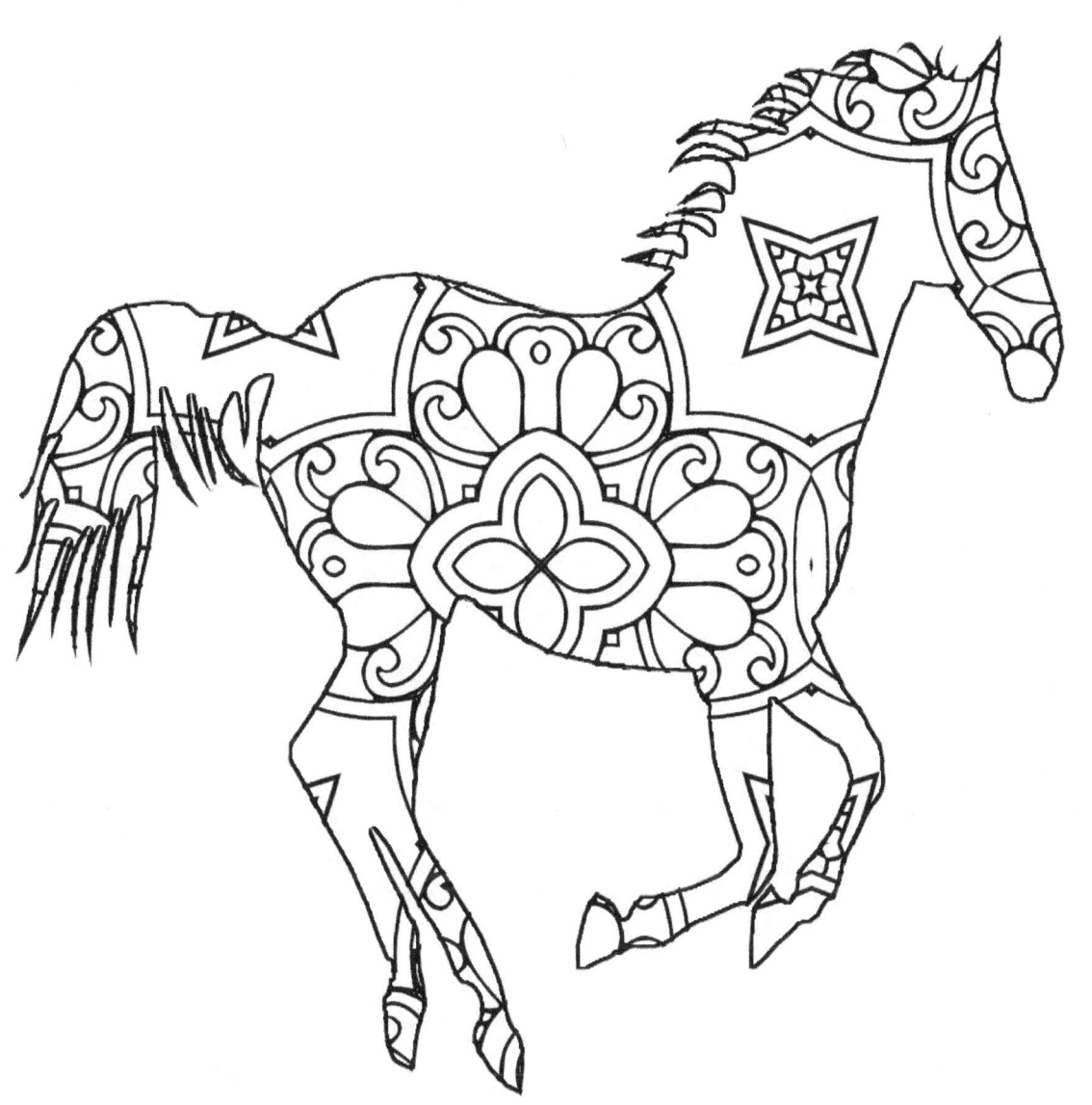

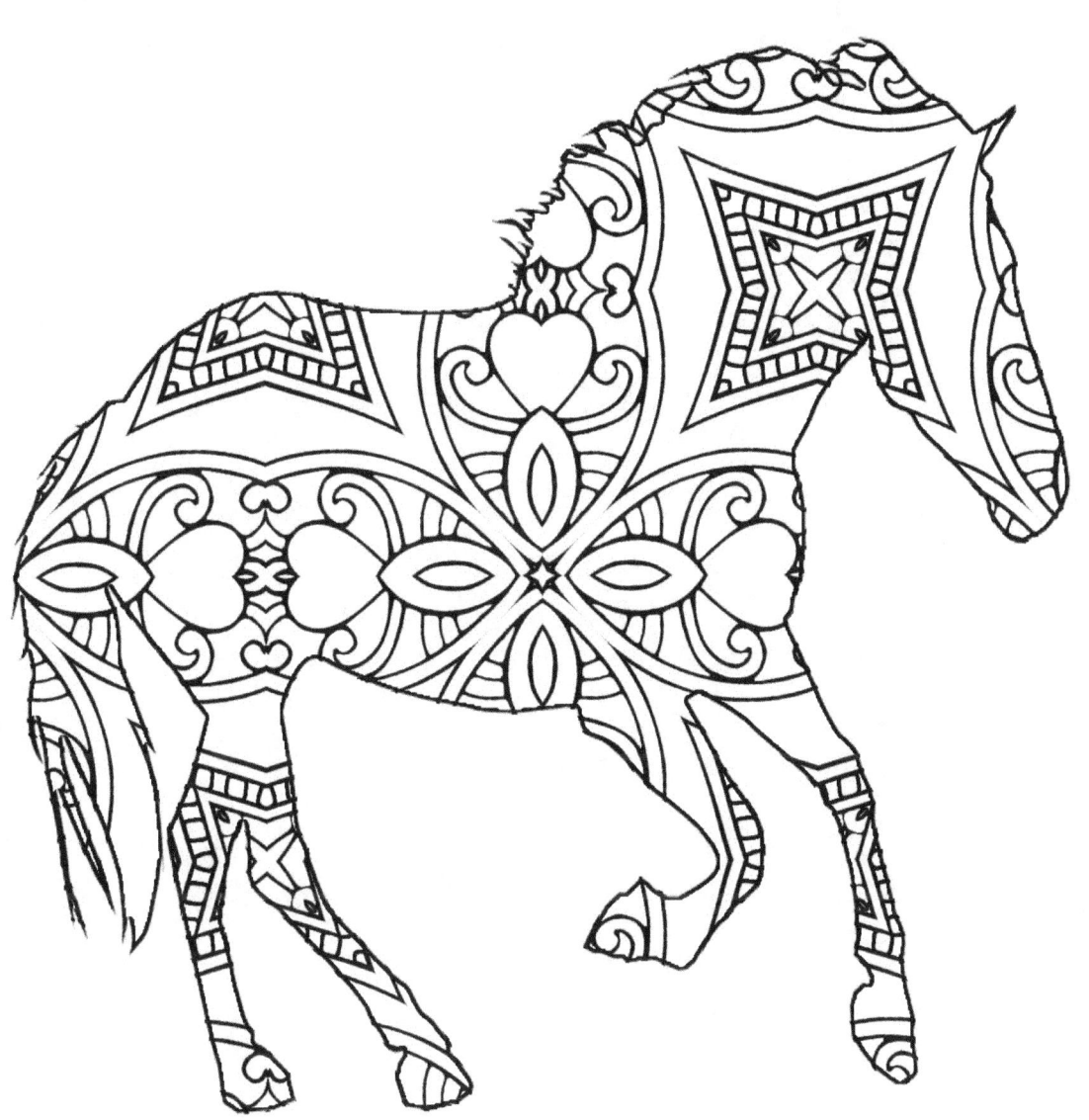

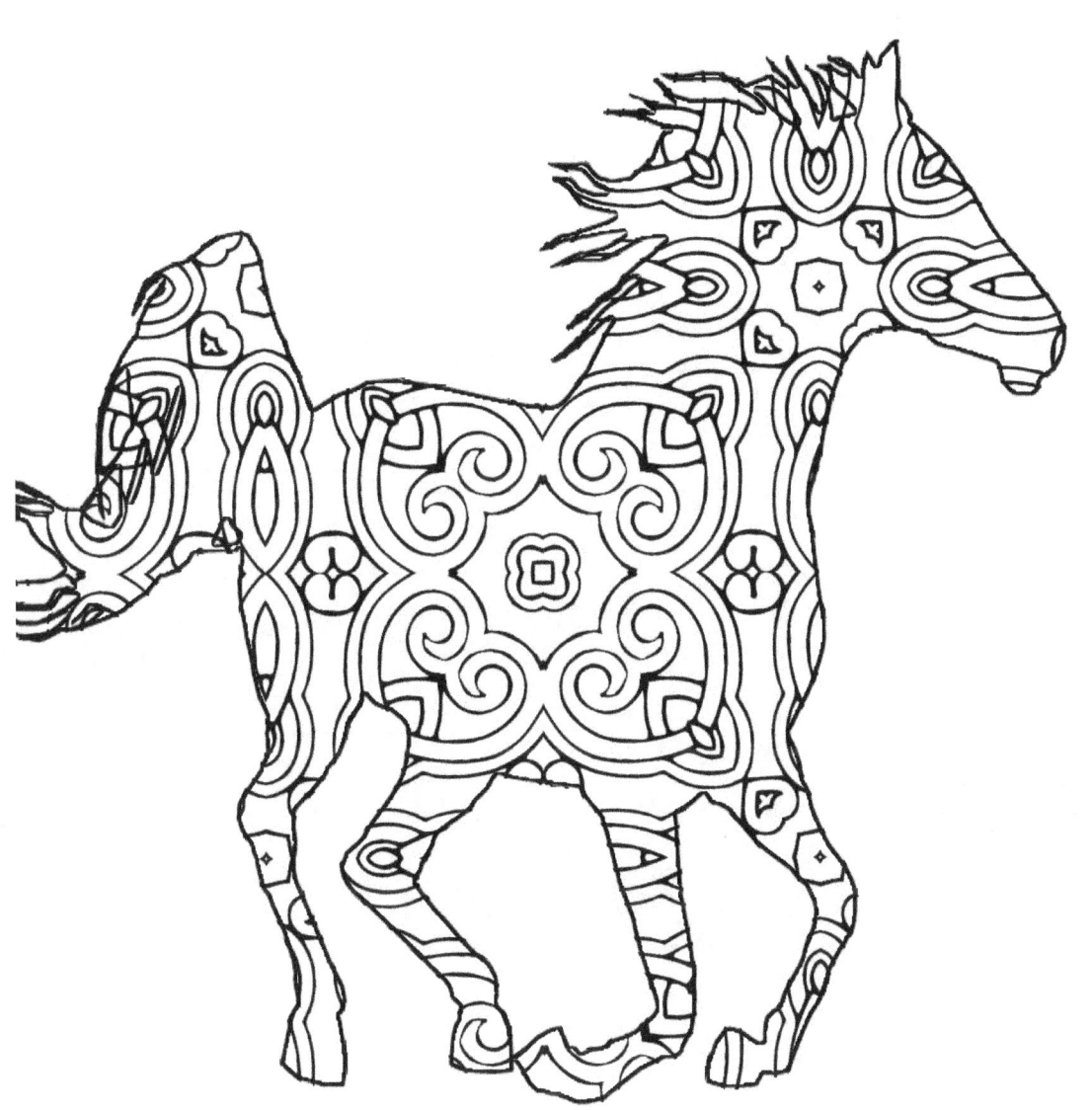

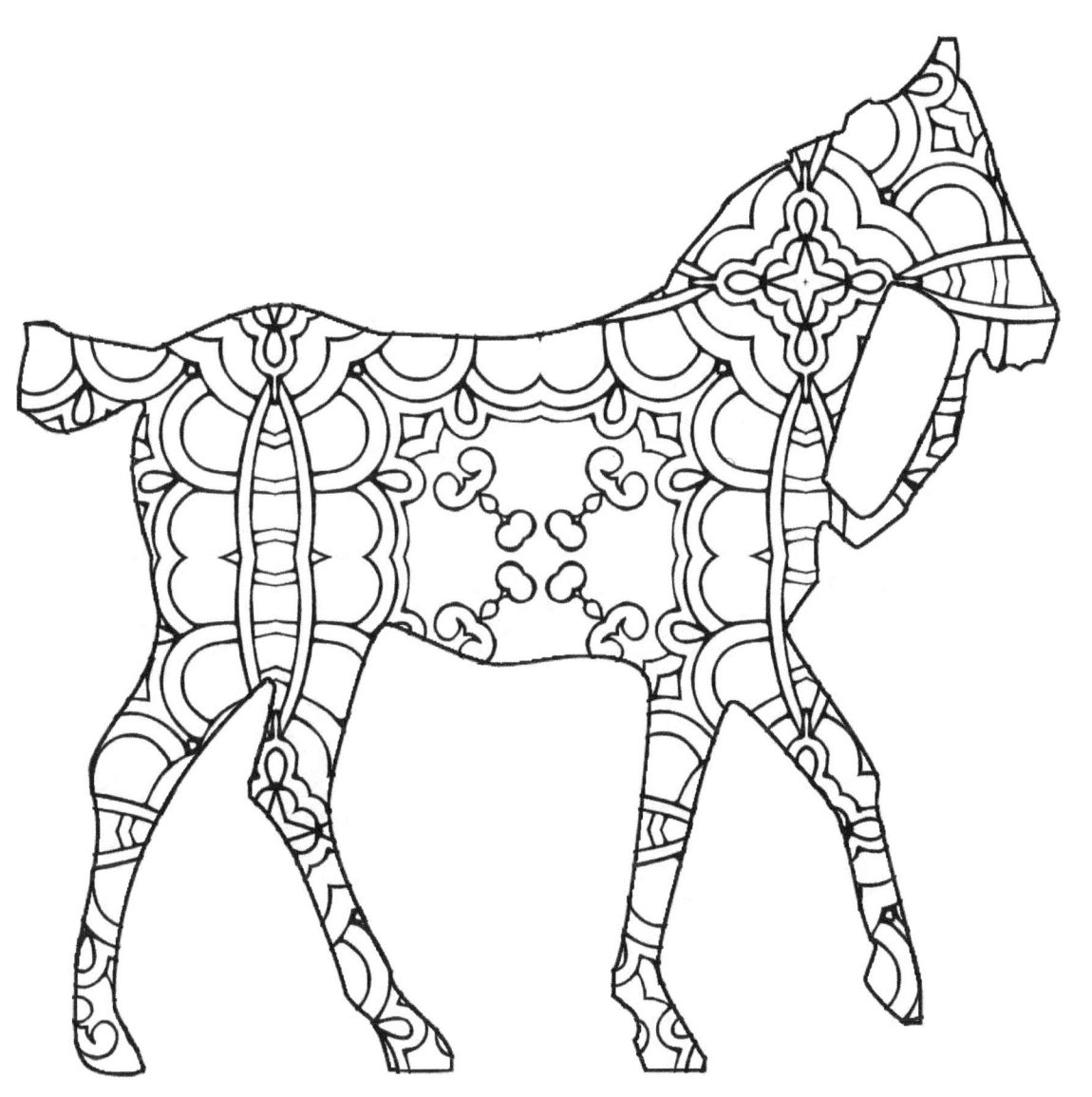

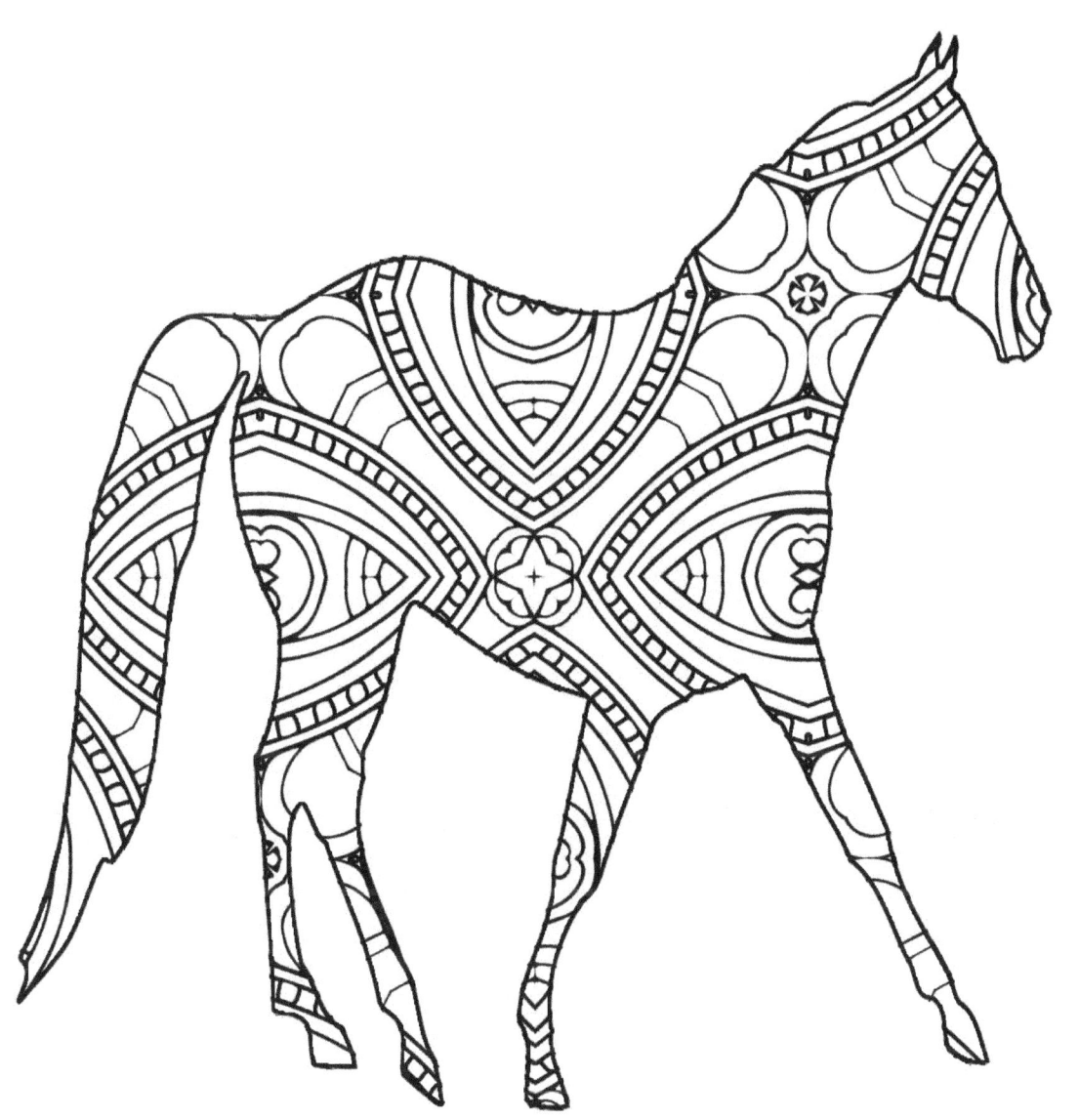

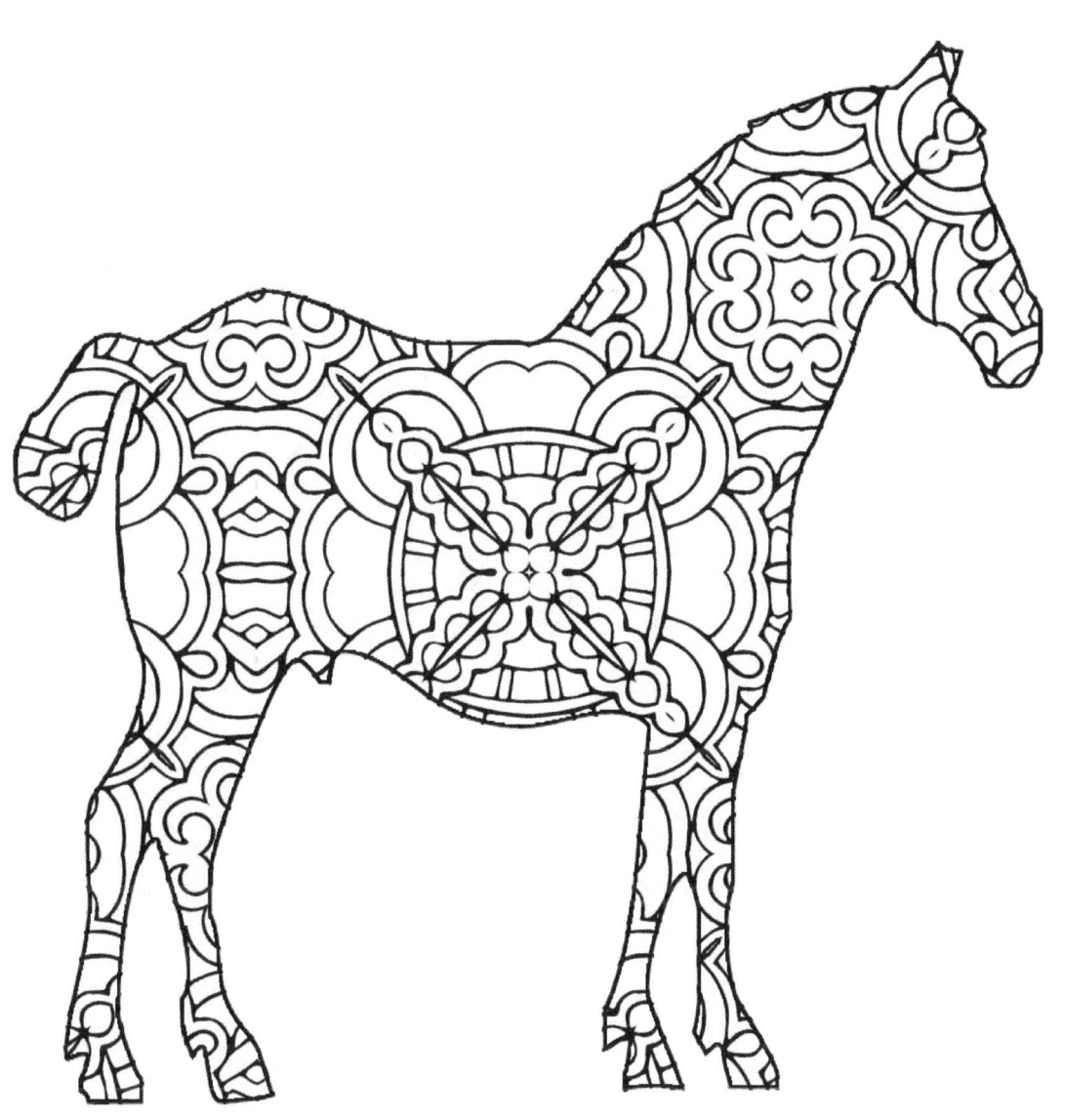

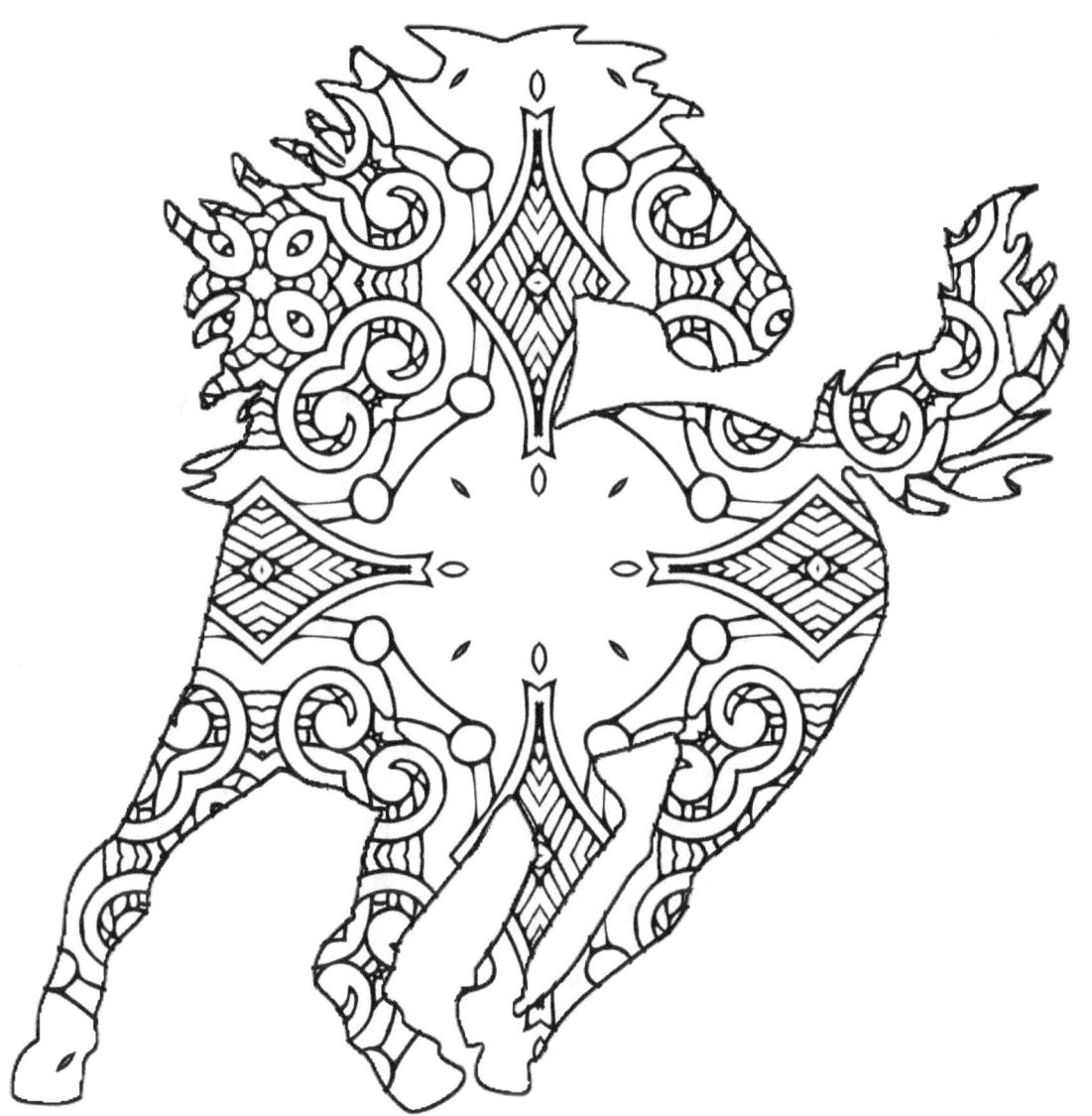

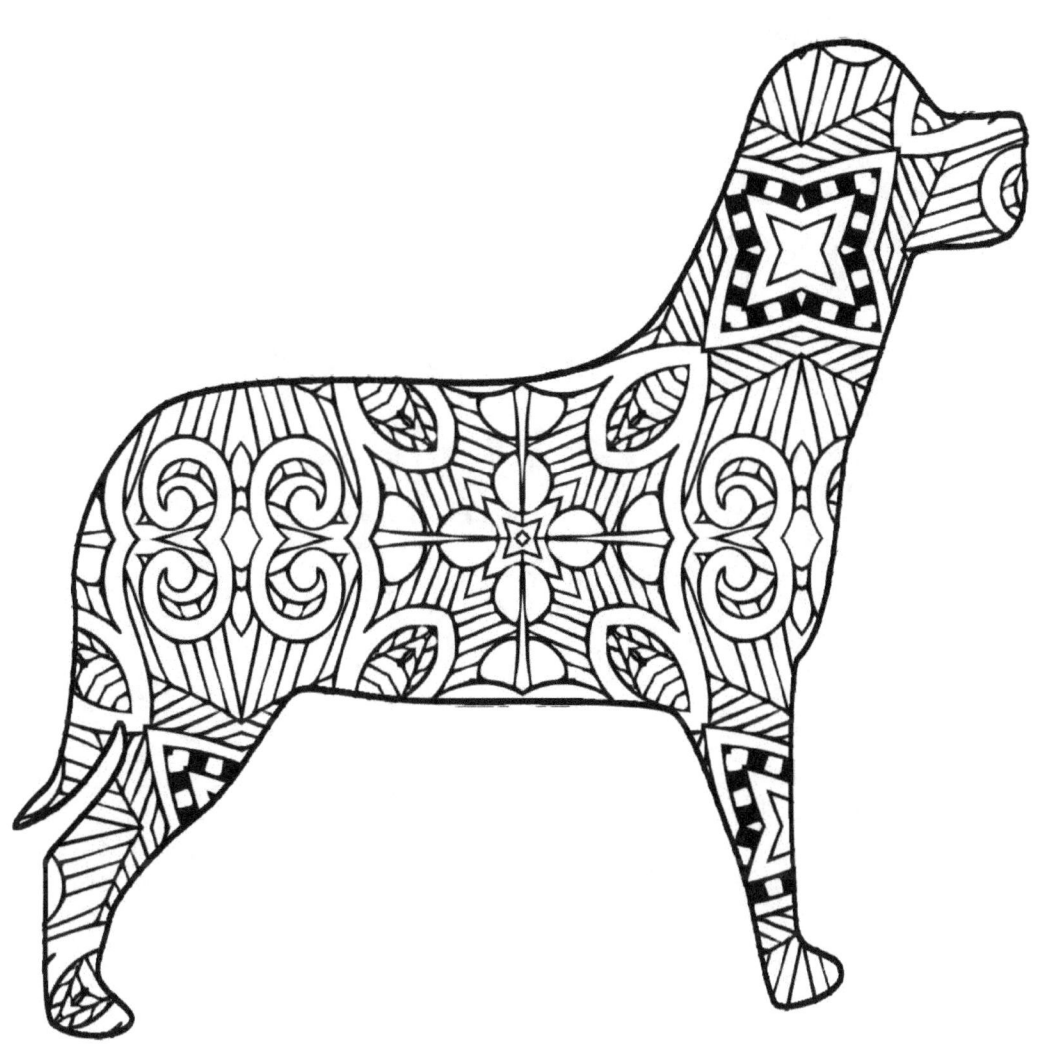

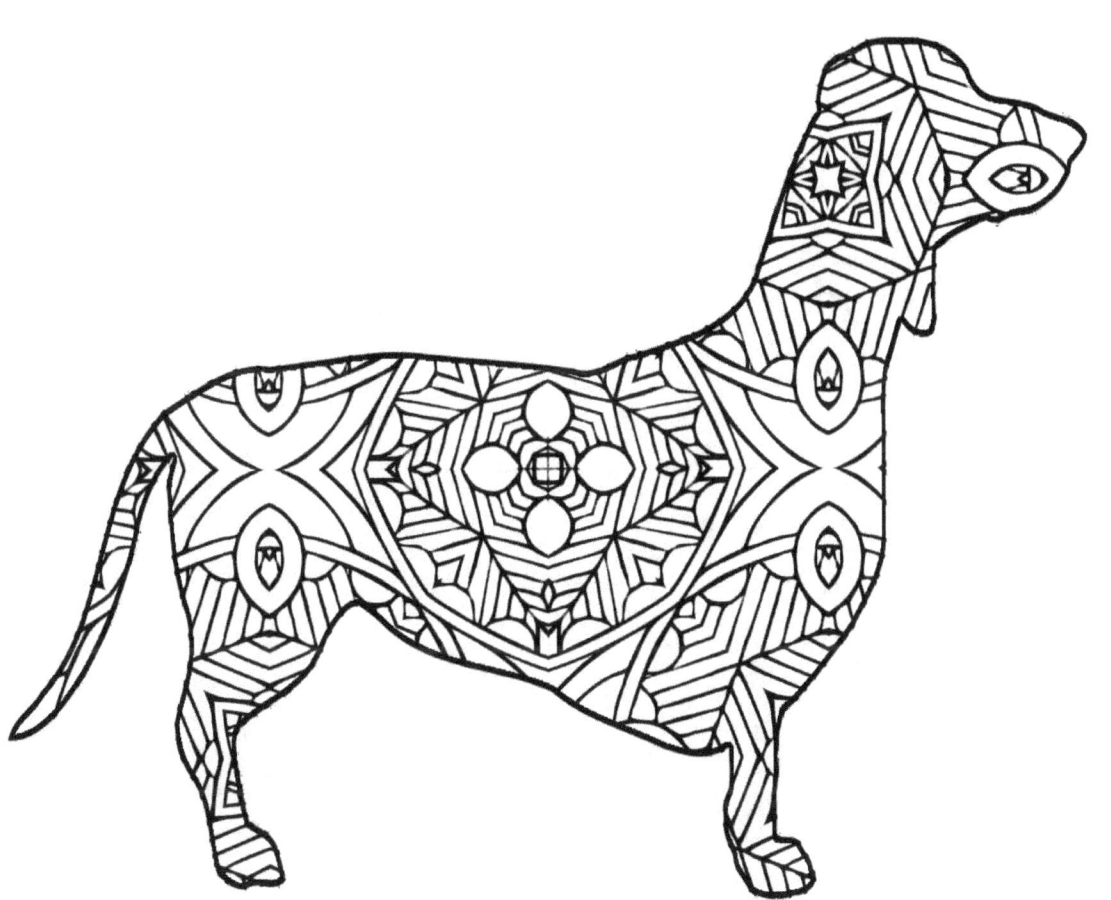

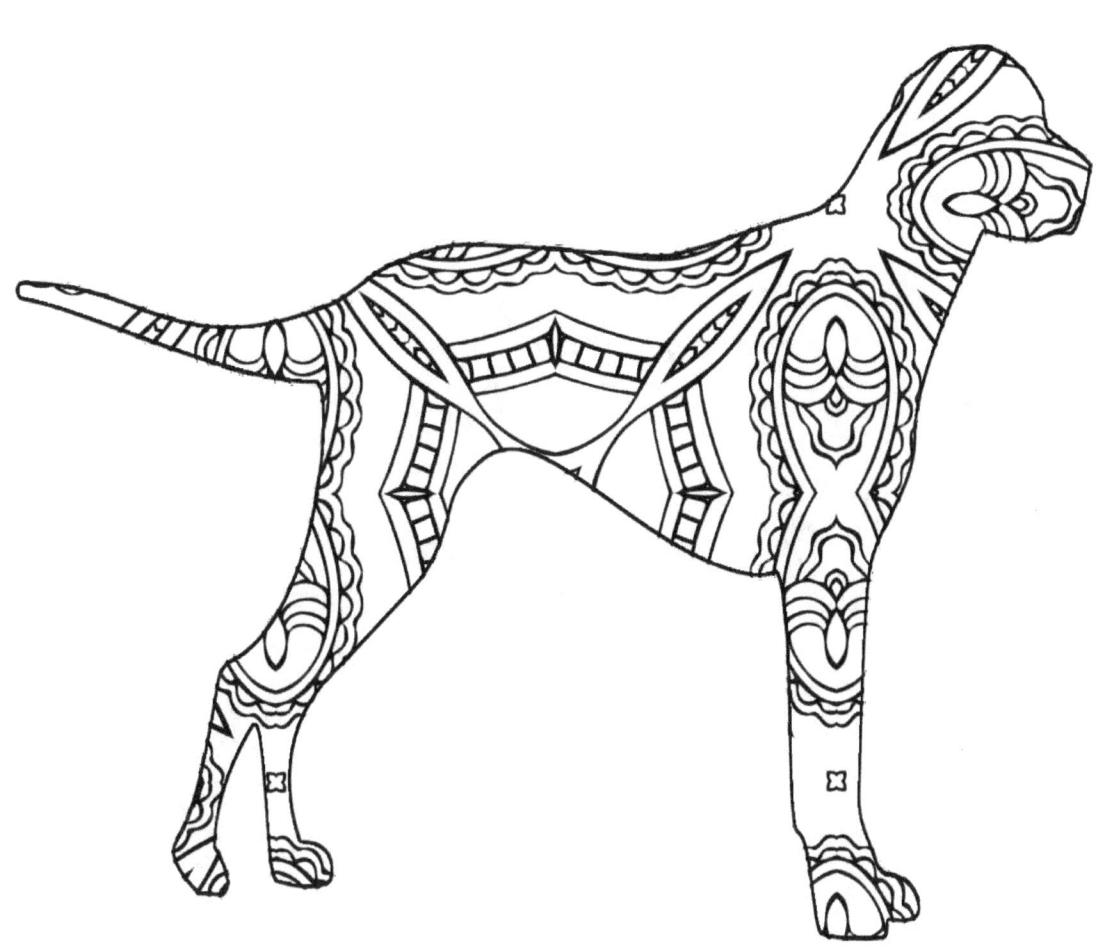

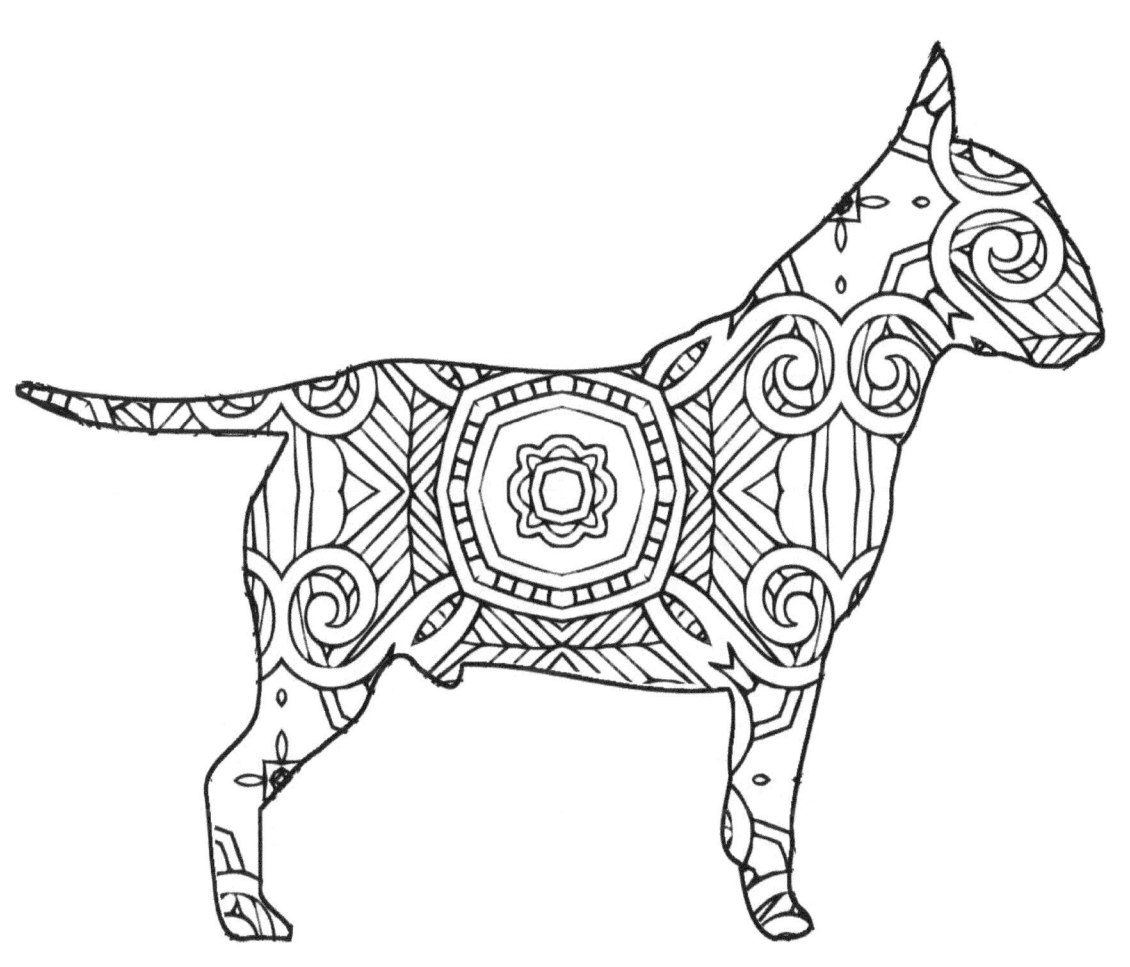

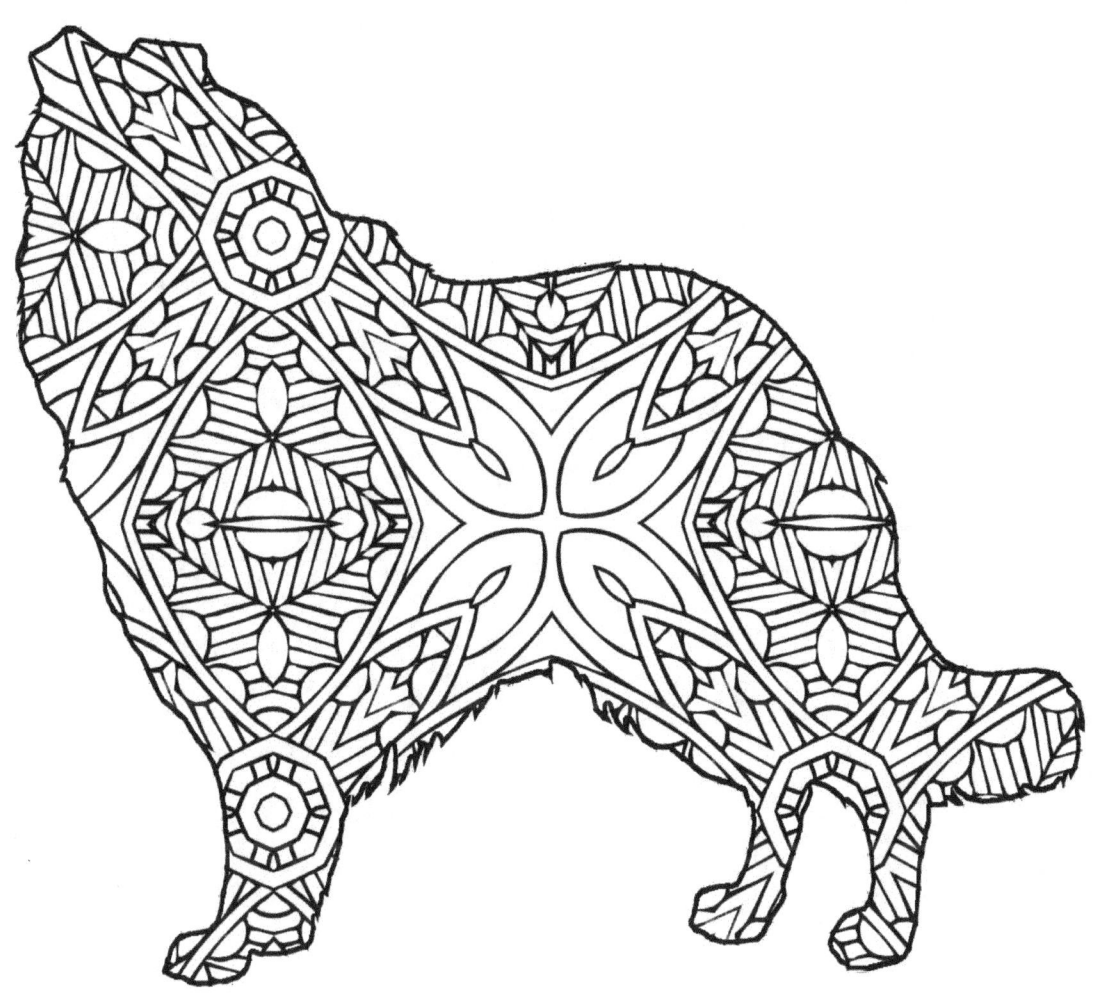

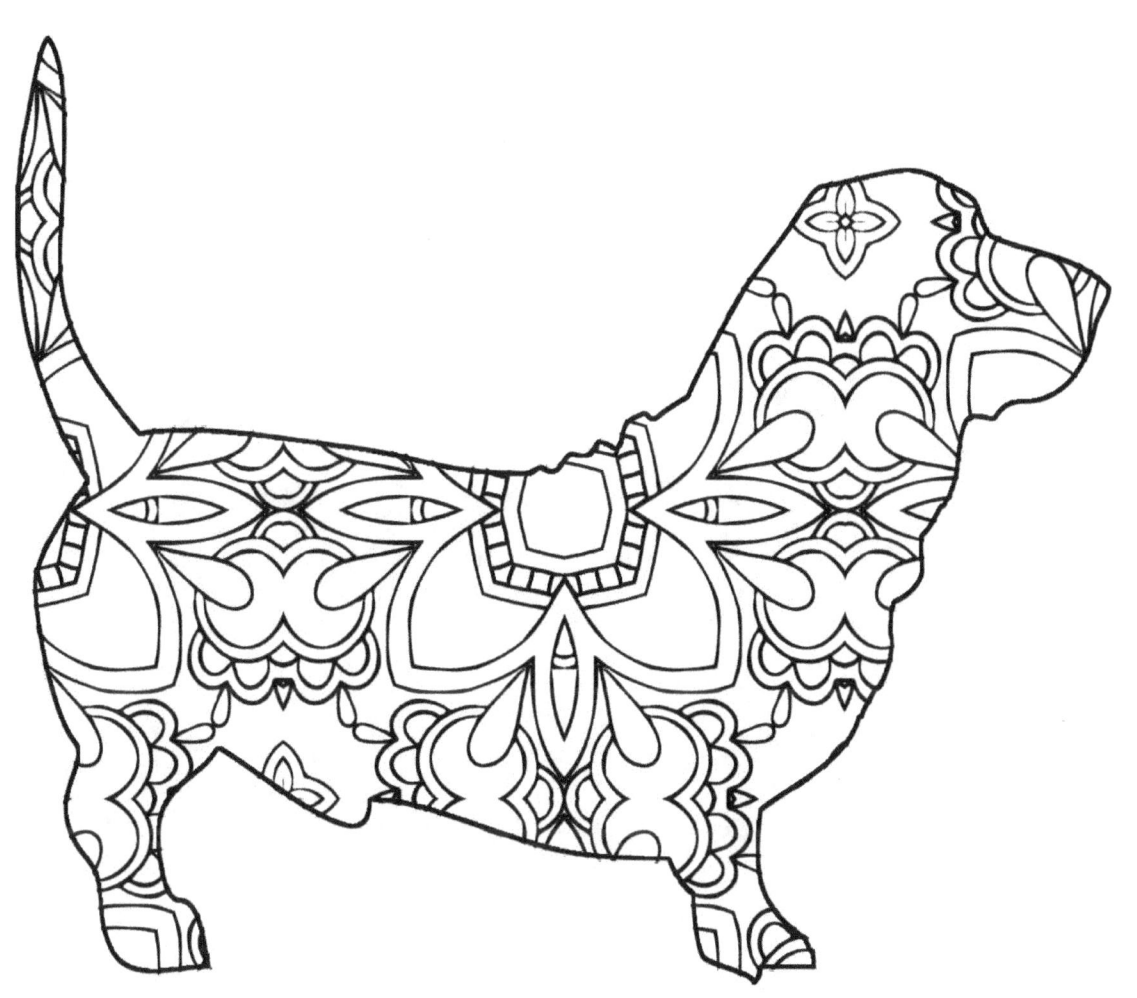

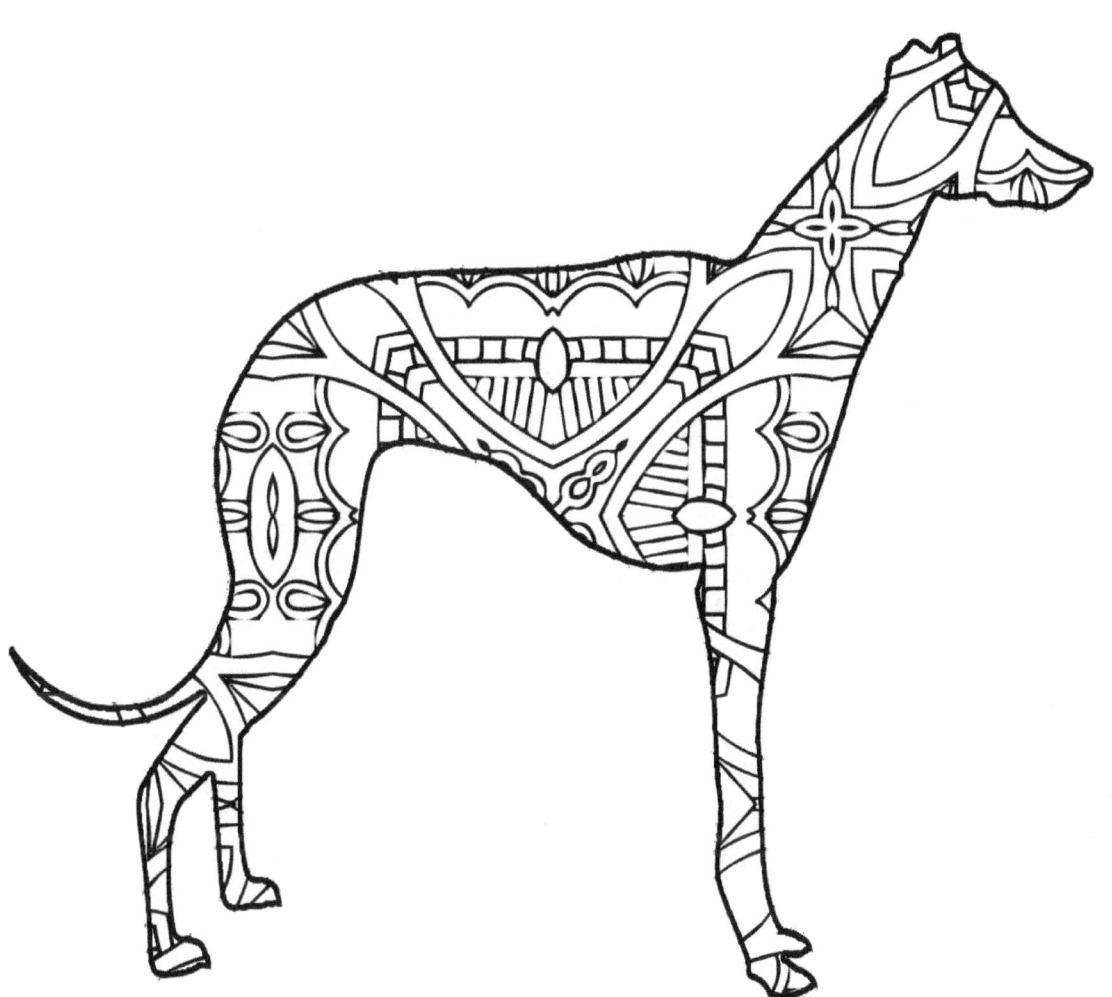

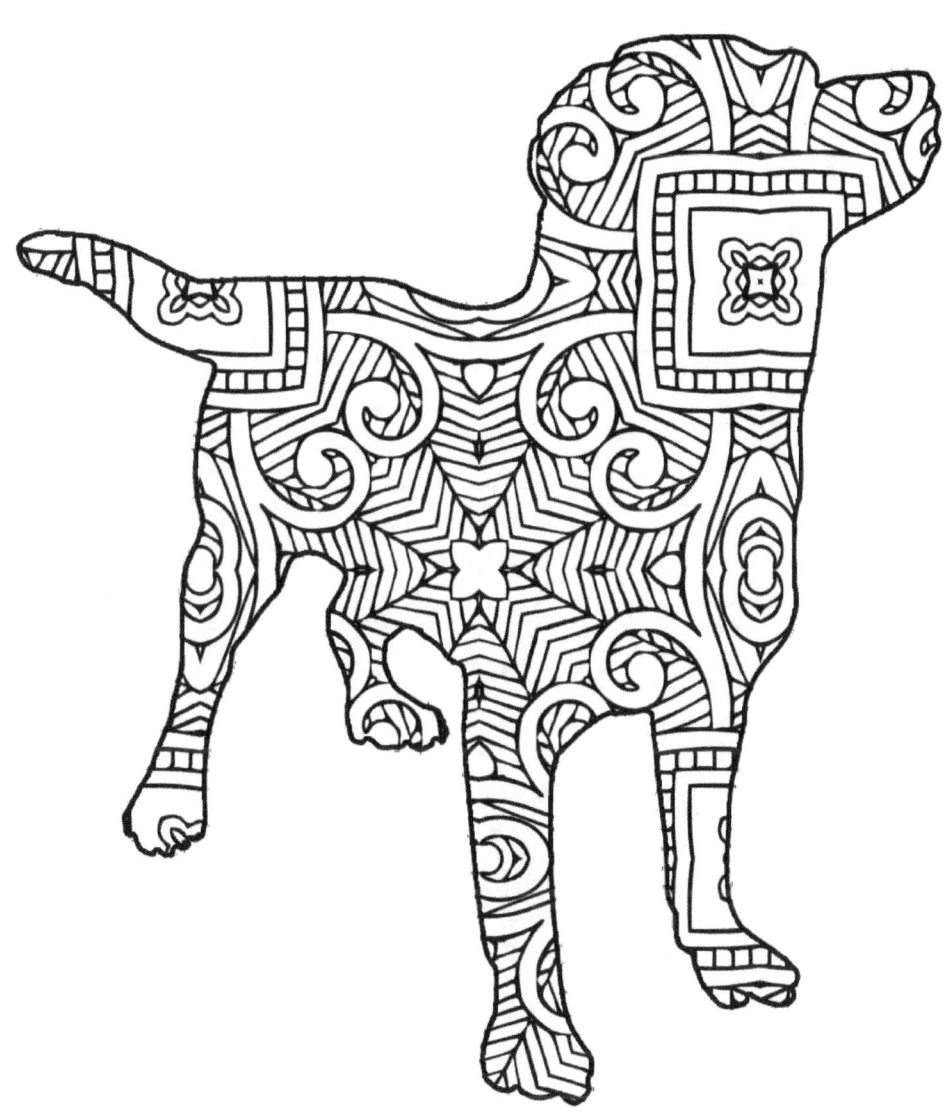

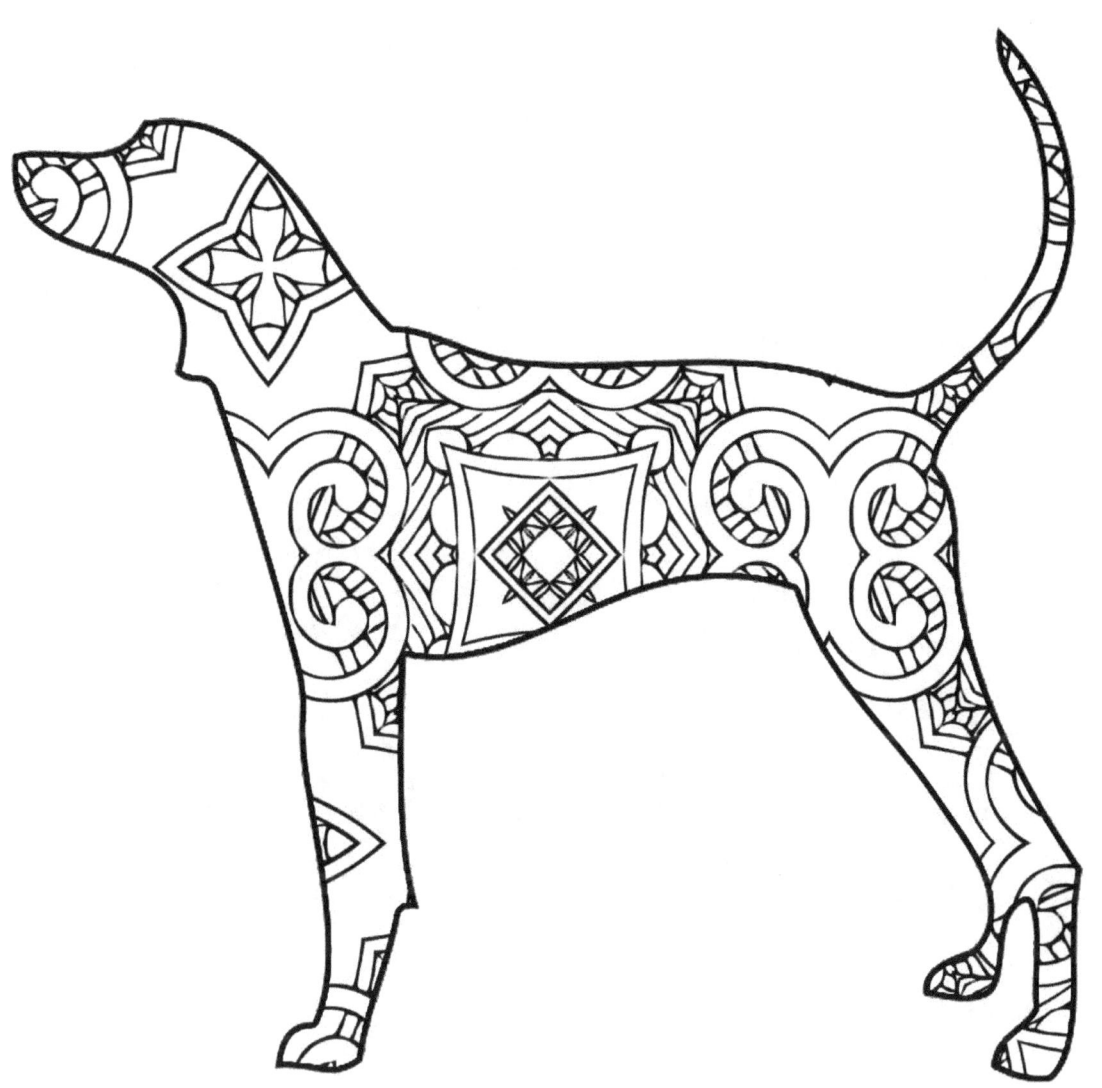

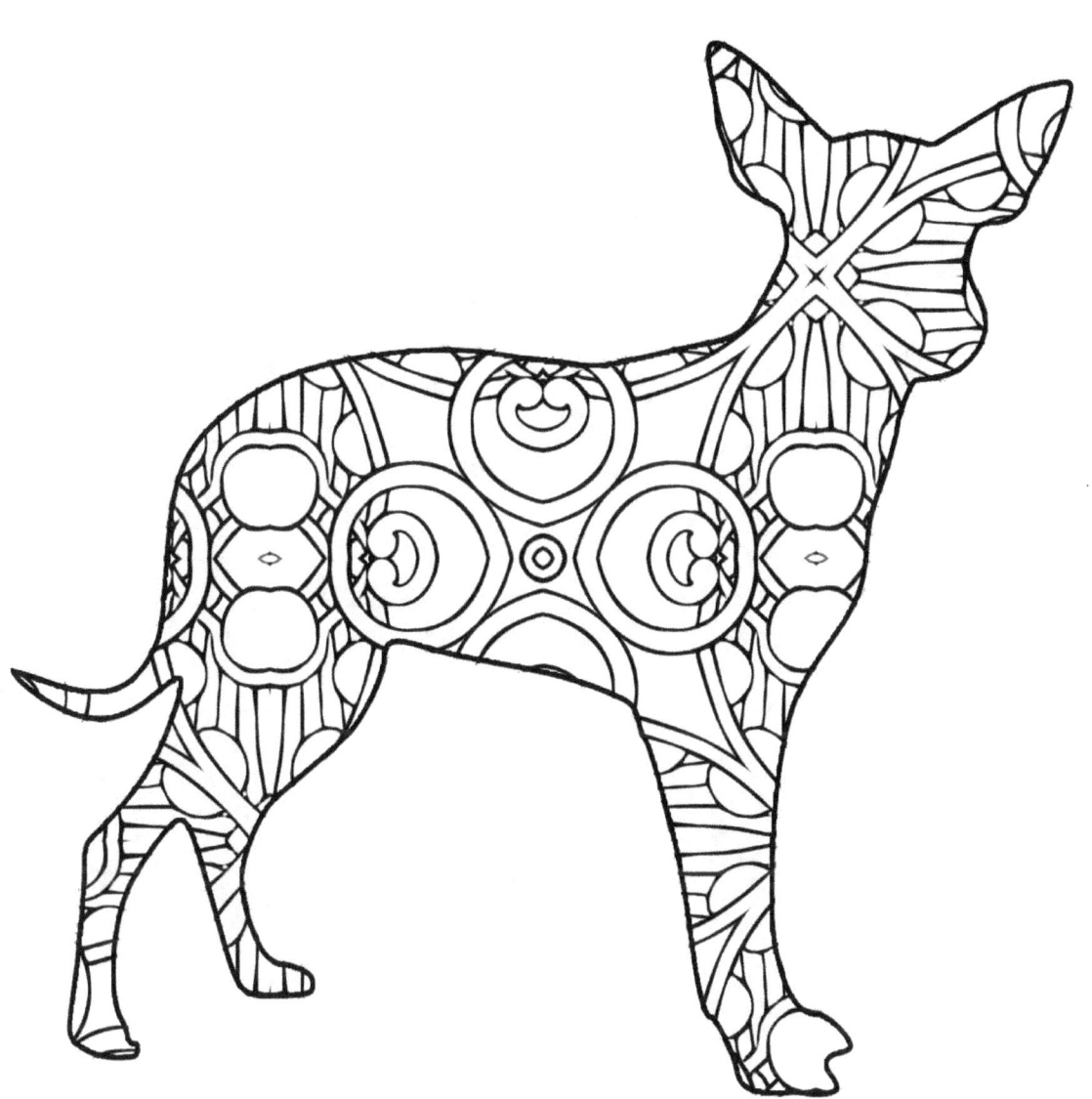

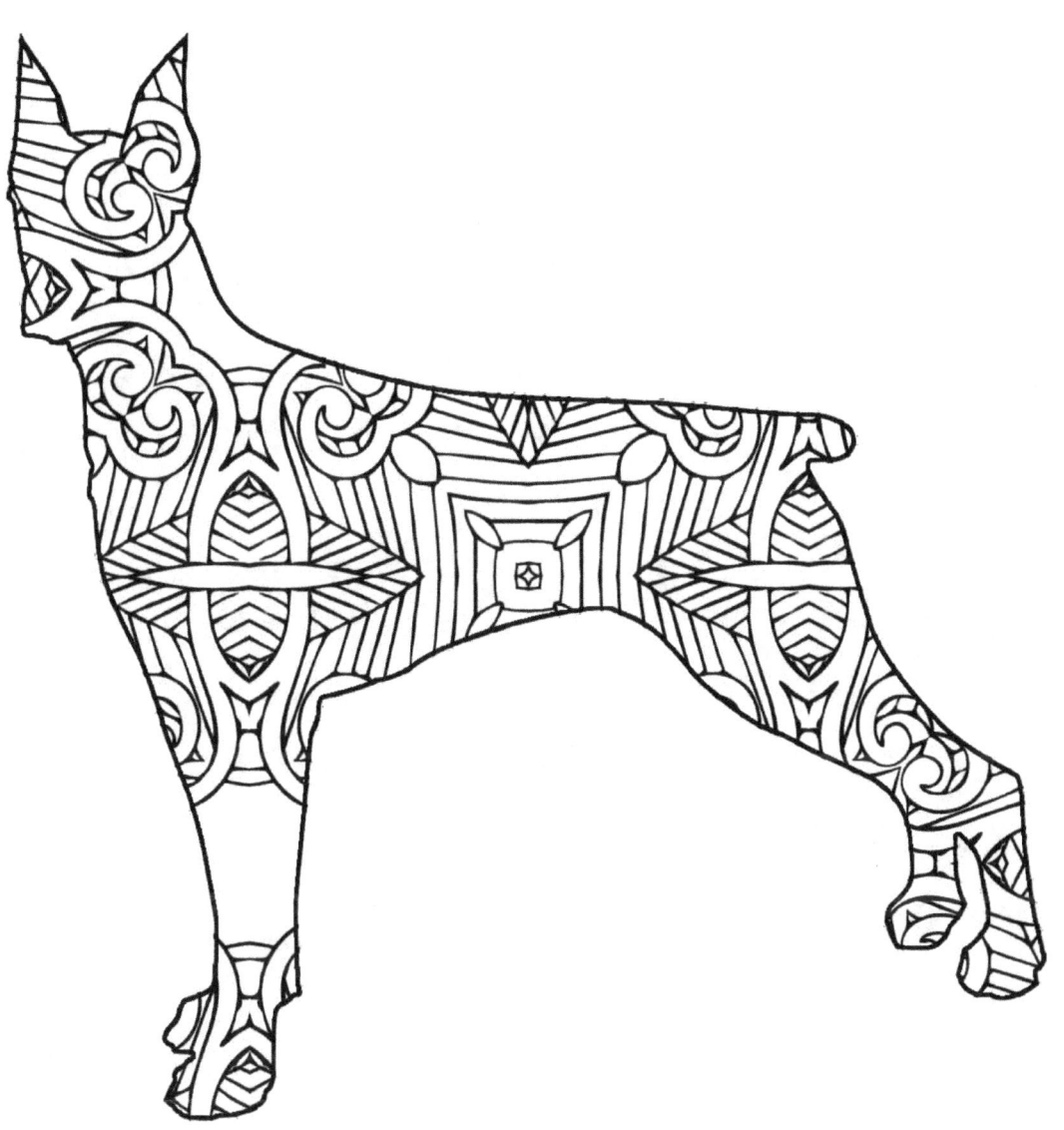

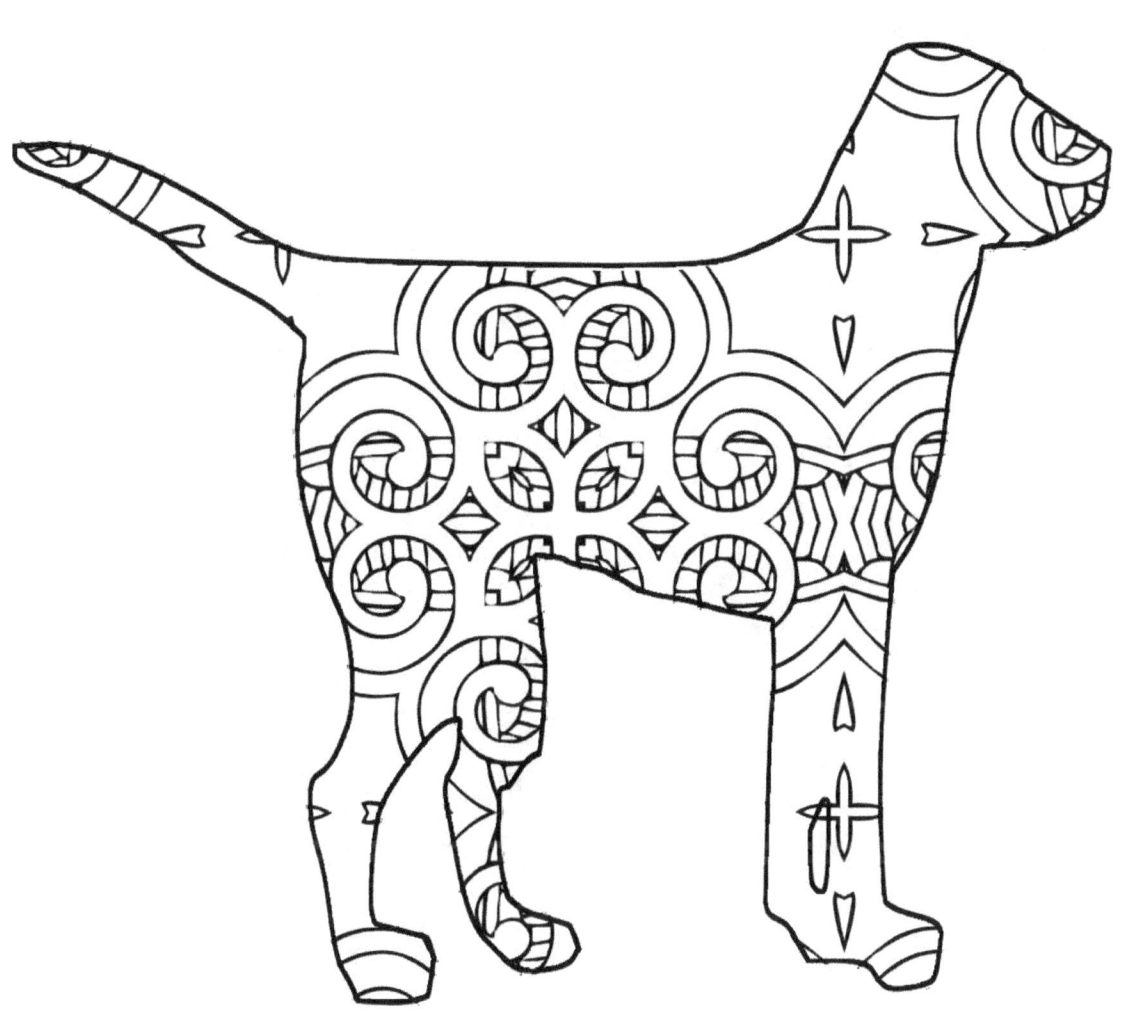

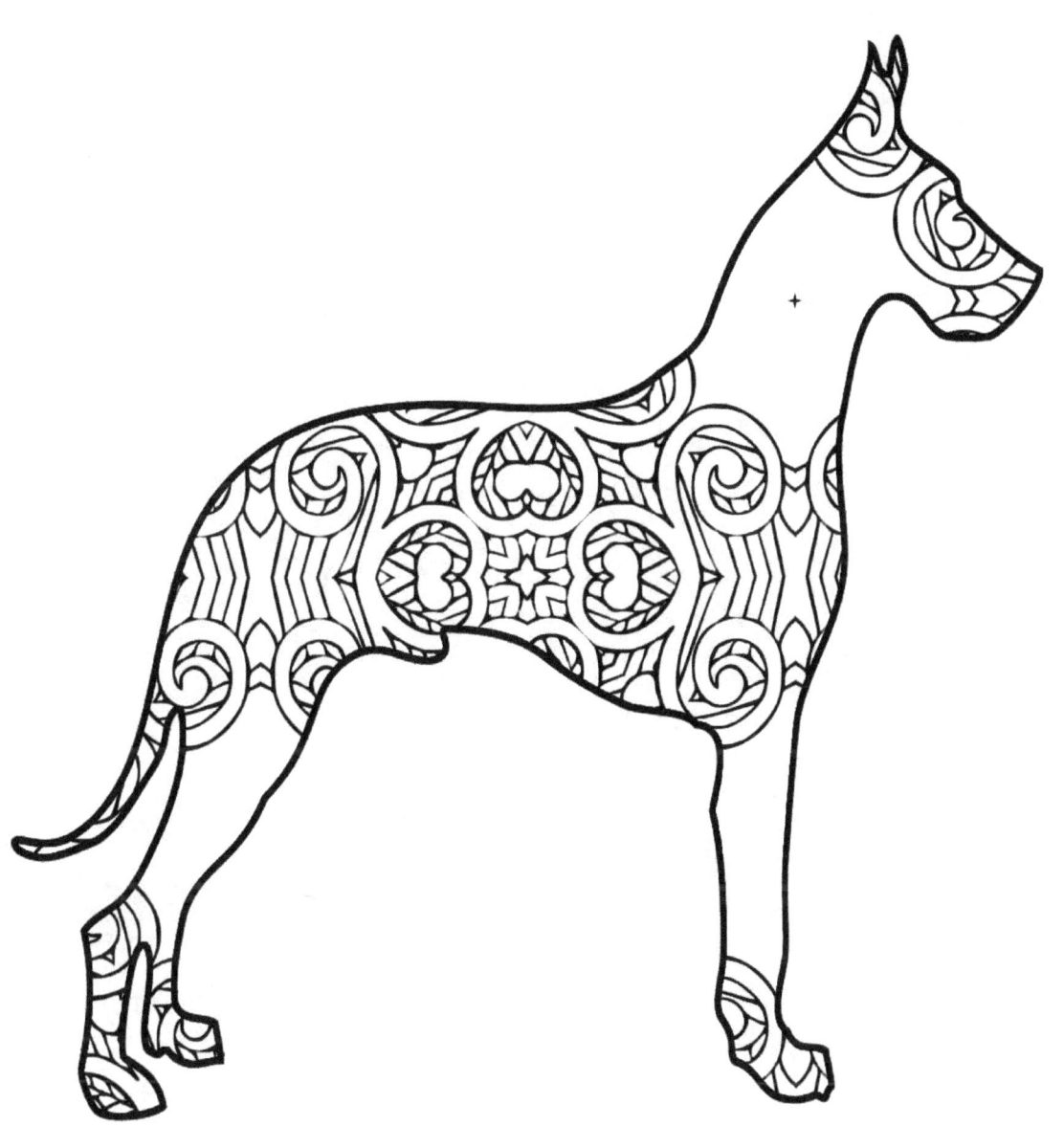

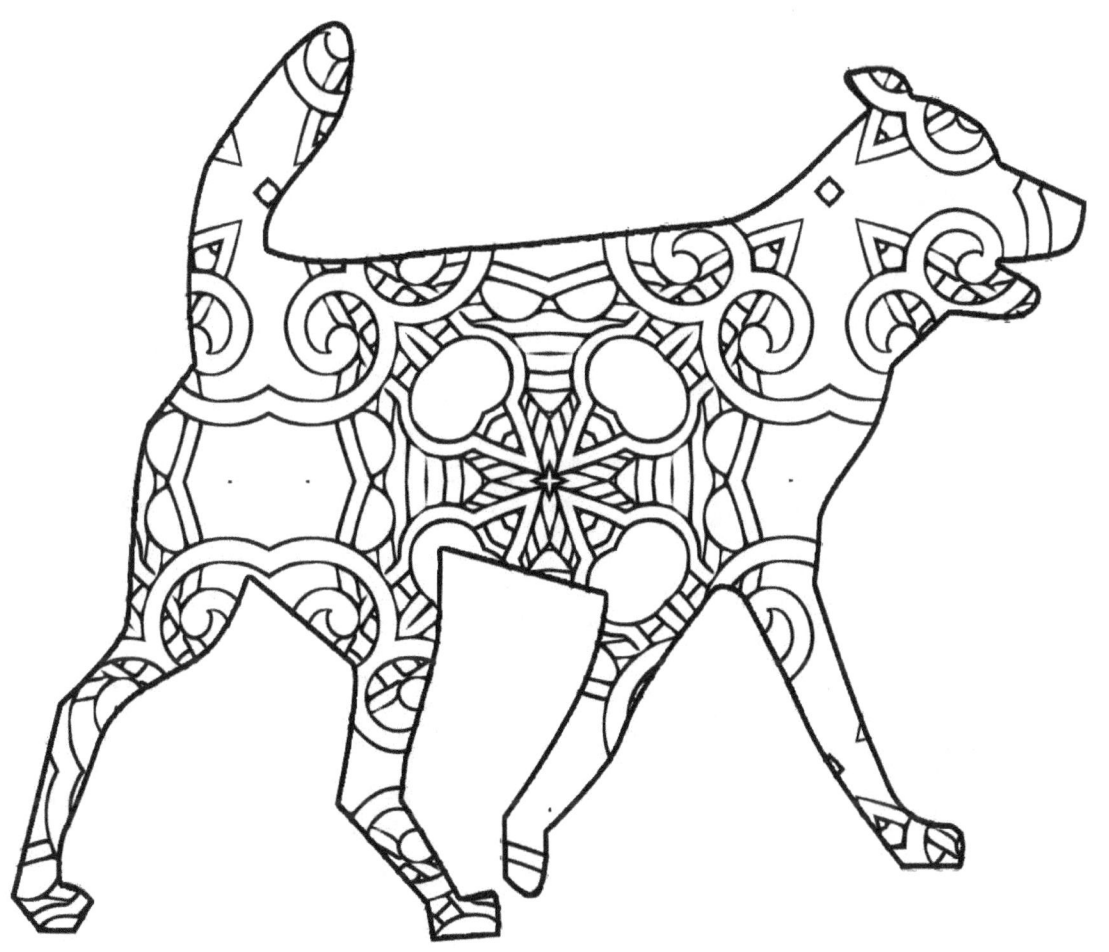

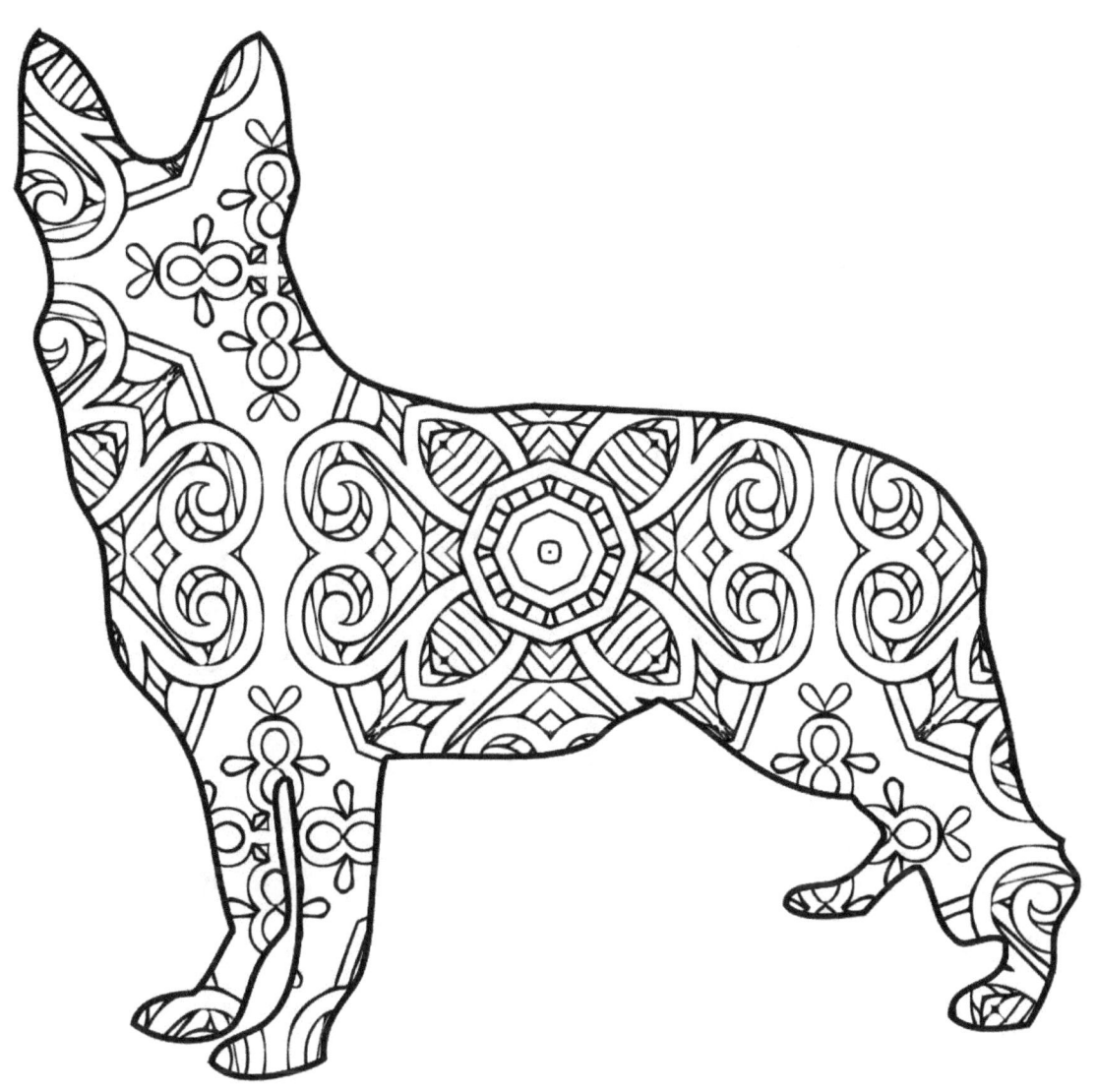

www.ingramcontent.com/pod-product-compliance
Lightning Source LLC
Chambersburg PA
CBHW081222170526
45165CB00009B/2917